Cover Image Representation

As you're probably aware, **the ancient, majestic bird, the mythical orange phoenix,** is **the universal symbol of transformation**.

And despite her angelic wings, Lady Phoenix is not a religious figure, nor a mythic goddess. But just as Lady Justice, with her blindfold and scales is the iconic symbol of the legal system; Lady Phoenix is **the iconic symbol of transformation — in human form.**

She's a symbolic metaphor for all of humanity, and especially victim/survivors, as she rises from the ashes of outdated paradigms and the past pain of abuse.

The Conscious Change Series of Books by Dr Stevie Carnegie

Bk 1 ~ Conscious Change for an Ethical Business, Life, and World: An Introduction to Conscious *We not Me* Change and the Conscious Change Series in Review

Bk 2 ~ Conscious Intelligence Competencies: Taking Emotional Intelligence to the Next Level for Our 21st Century World of Relationships ~ with Yourself and Others, in Business, with the Planet, and Beyond

Bk 3 ~ Conscious Self-Discovery: Your Key to a Happy, Loving, and Successful Life by Enriching Your Relationship with Yourself

Bk 4 ~ Conscious Life-Purpose: Live a Meaningful Life by "Making a Difference" for Greater Happiness, Love, and Success

Bk 5 ~ Conscious Love: Cultivating a Consciousness of Virtue-Based Love for a More Peaceful, Loving, and Sustainable World

Bk 6 ~ Conscious Gratitude: A Love-in-Action Virtue for Happiness, Health, and Loving Relationships at Home, at Work, and Around the World

Bk 7 ~ Conscious Feminine *ENERGY*: Beyond Gender, Toward Global Wisdom

Bk 7a~From Coercion to Courage: Rising from the Ashes of Past Pain and Outdated Paradigms

Bk 8 ~ Conscious Leadership: Born of Heart-Centred Life-Skills and Global Wisdom

Bk 9 ~ Conscious Happiness 101: Make Happiness a Habit with Positive Psychology, Play, Laughter, and Mindfulness Meditation

Bk 10 ~ Conscious Longevity: How to Live a Healthier, Happier, and Longer Life with an Understanding of Beneficial Nutrition and Appropriate Exercise ~ PLUS a Review of Exercise at Home Equipment

AND Their Prequel

BRAINWASHED: The True Story of Psychological Domestic Abuse and the PTSD Aftermath ~ with 10 International Book Awards

≈

Your Transformational Journey

To find out about your **Heart-Centred Conscious Leadership transformation** visit **Appendix A**, at the end of this book.

Be among the first to hear about the next intake of my online workshop

STRATEGIC HEART-CENTRED LEADERSHIP

ALSO

Download Your Free E-Book Now

Bk 1 ~ Conscious Change for an Ethical Business, Life, and World:

An Introduction to Conscious *We not Me* Change and the Conscious Change Series in Review

In just seven, short, fast-reading chapters you'll: ...

- ✓ Find out what "Conscious" Change is all about.
- ✓ Explore the Essential Keys for Genuine Heart-Centred "Conscious" Leadership and Conscious Intelligence.
- ✓ Find out how you too can become a Heart-Centred, "Conscious" Leader of Change in all areas of your life.
- ✓ Get an insight into the other books in the Conscious Change Series & your Transformational Journey.

To download now, just go to the following link

https://www.StevieCarnegie.com

From Coercion to Courage

Rising from the Ashes of Past Pain and Outdated Paradigms

Dr Stevie Carnegie

Book 7a – The Conscious Change Series of Books

From Coercion to Courage: Rising from the Ashes of Past Pain and Outdated Paradigms

Published via: https://www.ConsciousChangeToday.com

Cover Creation: Thanks to Aomar Omlil ~ https://www.fiverr.com/s/2KEq4wr

Paperback: ISBN: 978-1-7641026-3-6
Hardback: ISBN: 978-1-7641026-4-3

260308

Dedicated to

All Victim/Survivors of Abuse of any kind.

Remember, Surviving Takes Courage.

So the world is waiting for heroes like you.

Important Notes to Readers

AUSTRALIAN ENGLISH

This book is written in Australian/UK English. And so words like "colour" and "favourite" are spelled with a "u" included, and **Centre** is spelled with **"re"** at the end instead of **"er"—Center**. So, if you're from a non-Commonwealth country, I'll trust that you're open to diversity. And if not, then we really need to do some work together :-).

DISCLAIMER

All humans are very different and think and react in different ways to different issues. And if anything in this book raises any concerns for you, it's important that you talk with a good and appropriate healthcare professional.

USE OF "YOU"

Occasionally I use the 2nd person pronoun "you" in a generic 3rd person way, not because it necessarily applies to you specifically. So please don't take offence.

If this was an academic paper, I'd probably be using "one" as the 3rd person pronoun. For instance, one might say this, or one might do that. But I can't tell you how much this one hates that sort of language.

Book Description

From Coercion to Courage:

Rising from the Ashes of Past Pain and Outdated Paradigms

Coercion doesn't break bones.
It breaks identity.

Coercion isn't always loud. Often it's subtle. It creeps in through manipulation, threat, grooming, power imbalance, and a slow erosion of identity—tactics that turn "choice" into compliance, until you're no longer sure what you believe, what you feel, or even who you are. It's a power strategy that hijacks safety, consent, autonomy, and self-trust. It's psychological abuse. And psychological abuse can be fatal.

Here, **Dr. Stevie Carnegie** writes as both a survivor and a moral philosopher with a deep behavioural-science background. She unpacks coercion in a down-to-earth manner with uncommon clarity: the tactics, the traps, and the psychological mechanisms used to traumatise. And Stevie doesn't just describe trauma; she explains what it can do to the brain, to trust, to identity, and to a person's future choices.

From Coercion to Courage is a moral mirror held up to modern life.

Using **the #MeToo movement** as a touchstone, you'll explore the lived reality of coercive control and sexual coercion in workplaces and communities, and the psychological aftermath that can linger for a lifetime.

You'll also see coercion at scale through **the Epstein Files**—how institutions and cultures of entitlement protect the powerful, blame the victims, and quietly normalise what should never be normal—leaving the wounded to carry the shame and their invisible scars.

Stevie tells the truth plainly enough that even the skeptics can't wriggle out of it.

A system that fails victims is not merely flawed—it's ethically compromised.

Then comes **the turning point: transformation**. The quiet **courage** of reclaiming your life. **The courage** to speak, to heal, to rebuild boundaries and choose your next chapter. Survivors don't need pity. They need their self-trust back. They need identity back. They need a future they can stand inside without fear.

This book is not about revenge. It's **a call for personal rebirth** and **institutional reform**. It's about truth. It's about the ethical courage to follow the path forward.

And sadly, coercion isn't rare.

It's just rarely named. And what we don't name,

we can't change.

Table of Contents

~ Chapter 1 ~
Brainwashed

Virtually anyone can be negatively brainwashed, coerced or psychologically abused, into doing almost anything.
It's not your fault.

~ Katie ~ DV Survivor ~

Some time ago, I thought my book ***Brainwashed*** was finished—done and dusted—with so much of the trauma, pain, and memories behind me. But fast forward to the end of 2025, and it all began replaying like a cracked record.

Why?

Well, towards the end of 2025 one of the main news stories items was about the release of the so-called, **Epstein Files.** These are an extremely large mob of documents, emails, photographs and videos compiled by the infamous multi-millionaire sex offender Jeffrey Epstein, his associates/playmates, and the many FBI files on the case.

I don't intend to go into the deeply disturbing, despicable, details about Epstein, or his major sex trafficking operation of under-aged girls and young women, to some of the richest and highest profile men around the world. However, the article in this Endnote[1] will give you a broad overview, if you're not sure what went on.

But my need to say something here, at this time is due to all too many members of the public being totally unaware of what a serious subject **coercion is**, and what it's all about. This is clearly being demonstrated by the **victim-blaming comments** I've seen and heard expressed towards many of those young girls and women who were allegedly trafficked by Epstein.

On the one hand, I see and hear comments like, "how horrific" that under-aged girls were sex-trafficked. And that is so very true.

On the other hand, I see and hear all too many insensitive, ignorant, and arrogant comments like, these girls might have been under the legal age of consent, but they were old enough to know what to do and were paid for their "favours". So surely they were all just young prostitutes.

Now I could write a long ethical analysis on negative attitudes to your so-called "average prostitute" versus any young woman who has a one night stand with a man she's just met, in return for being taken out to an expensive dinner.

But I'll leave those analyses for another forum.

Instead, I knew I had to add another chapter to my book, ***Brainwashed.*** A new chapter that was defending all abuse victim/survivors, not only of Jeffrey Epstein and his playmates, but of **ALL abuse**, including the often hidden psychological or emotional abuse, as I experienced.

More often than not, it's psychological abuse that leads to a victim/survivor being so **vulnerable to coercion and future abuse**. As you'll shortly discover, psychological or emotional, abuse is often the precursor to physical abuse and even homicide—or perhaps more appropriately femicide.

Just as I did in my ***Brainwashed*** book, I needed to explain to those lucky enough to have never been abused, what so many victim/survivors of abuse go through.

That new ***Brainwashed*** chapter was primarily on the very **misunderstood topic of Coercion** and how victim/survivors—not only female, but also male and non-binary—can have a new life, not **DESPITE** of the abuse, but **BECAUSE** of the abuse.

Once finished, I decided that it was such an important topic that I needed to reproduce an expanded version of that new ***Brainwashed*** chapter. And that I've done here, in the form of this stand-alone book, ***From Coercion to Courage,*** that can be quickly and easily read, and passed around to others.

It's my sincere hope that this book will give victim/survivors the strength to speak up, speak out, and thrive.

So here, Chapters 1 – 4, are the essential foothills, preparing you for the climb to the summit of the topic on coercion.

You begin your climb in Chapter 5 ~ "2017 #MeToo" and Chapter 6 ~ "The Epstein Files" as you're introduced to some major global examples of coercion-in-action, that I'm sure will be familiar to you.

And Chapter 7, "What Would You Do... ***REALLY?***" is the summit of the exposé on coercion, where you'll find some important insights to reflect on.

Then in Chapters 8 and 9, you're on your transformational journey where you'll be shown how victim/survivors, can reclaim their authentic identity. **Yes, a transformational rebirth is possible for anyone who wants it.**

But before starting our coercion exposé, I'd just like to give you an overview of my multi-award-winning book, ***Brainwashed,*** so that you have some idea of how this relatively short book fits in with the much longer 456 pages of ***Brainwashed***.

Brainwashed: *The True Story of Psychological Domestic Abuse and the PTSD Aftermath,* is not only the true story of my survival and the science behind it, but it's also the prequel to my Conscious Change Series of 10 books. In Appendix A, you'll find a brief summary of those 10 books, and how they can guide **"Your Transformational Journey"**.

And so I call this book, **Book 7a** in the Conscious Change series, because it's **a bridge between Book 7** ~ ***Conscious Feminine ENERGY,*** where you're introduced to the transformational work of Lady Phoenix, **and Book 8** ~ ***Conscious***

Leadership with Lady Phoenix on the cover, with her wings removed (aka sleeves rolled up) ready to guide your transformation with her Lady Phoenix ***ENERGY***.

In describing ***Brainwashed***, I like to begin with the line I often use, **"Sometimes, We Just Don't Know Who Our Greatest Enemy Is"**. That's because as children we don't know what we don't know. So initially, ***Brainwashed*** focuses, obviously on brainwashing, especially in relation to **childhood conditioning** which can be either positive or negative, or a combination of both. But when it's negative, it's a form of psychological abuse.

Psychological Abuse, including coercive control, gaslighting, weaponizing niceness, and insidious brainwashing is one of the most misunderstood epidemics of our time, whether perpetrated in an office, a church, a school, the community, or a family home. It leaves no visible scars, yet it can lead to disastrous, even deadly, decisions, lasting trauma, physical brain damage, and full-blown PTSD, unless it's **named, understood,** and **"healed"**.

For decades, I believed I'd had a good childhood.

Why?

No bruises. No overt violence. But when the wounds are invisible, so is the understanding, even by the victims themselves.

So it was decades later, that I uncovered the truth: **my greatest enemy had always been the invisible, psychological abuse** I'd suffered growing up—abuse that trained me to accept as "normal" an emotionally devastating toxic marriage, disguised as love.

I eventually realised the only way to help the public understand this hidden plague of emotional/psychological abuse was to expose it while telling my own story. It took time and courage, but eventually, almost as a form of therapy, and healing, I told my story in ***Brainwashed.***

As I explain in Chapter 1 of ***Brainwashed,*** initially, I received an enormous number of negative comments about me, personally, and my actions. Just as so many Epstein victims today are being victim-blamed. It was clear that unless someone had actually experienced the life that victim/survivors have endured, **they just did not get it—they couldn't fully understand.**

As I said a moment ago, **when the wounds are invisible, so is the understanding.**

My answer to this came from the comment I received from one of my original reviewers (***Brainwashed,*** Chapter 1). They said: "It might have been different if you'd been sitting beside me as I read through the book. I could then have asked questions, and **you could have explained why** you agreed to do the things you did."

I then knew what I had to do. I rewrote ***Brainwashed*** as if I was doing that exact thing.

Using my decades of behavioural science, and neuroscience research, I explained in a very down-to-earth manner, why I did what I did, bit-by-bit, as I told my story.

I was able to shatter myths and answer some of the real WHY questions including:

- Why "just leave" isn't as easy as the armchair critics like to believe.
- Why psychological abuse is so often missed, dismissed, or misunderstood, even by the victim/survivors themselves.
- Why trauma is not "just a psychological issue" —it can leave deep and measurable brain damage, without even a finger placed on the victim.
- Why psychological trauma, and resulting PTSD, can be fatal—setting aside the all too many suicides it leaves in its wake.
- Why subsequent trauma can have catastrophic consequences.

- And how true, lasting, soul-deep healing becomes possible—***IF*** the right people come along.

So *Brainwashed* is no ordinary memoir.

Today, ***Brainwashed*** is a rallying cry for **recognition, understanding,** and **change** because my story is true for more people than is realised. And it's certainly true for all the Epstein victim/survivors.

And **my greatest enemy could well be your greatest enemy too, in some form**.

So ***Brainwashed*** takes you inside the anatomy of toxic power, explaining the **WHAT** and the **WHY** of abuse—**the Anatomy.**

However, it's important to realise that there is an antidote to abuse. And you'll find that in my Conscious Leadership work.

Conscious Leadership: *Born of Heart-Centred Life-Skills and Global Wisdom* (Bk 8 in the Conscious Change Series) and my "Strategic Heart-Centred Leadership" workshop uncovers the **HOW** to overcome the effects of abuse—through **Courage, Compassion, Creativity**, and **Conscious Intelligence.**

Because the same **abusive toxic patterns of behaviour** seen destroying a childhood, or a marriage, can also poison a business, an organisation, or an entire culture. And so throughout this book, ***From Coercion to Courage,*** please be open to the many times I'll speak about repeated "**patterns of behaviour**".

***Brainwashed* – the anatomy of abuse;**

***Conscious Leadership* –the antidote;**

***From Coercion to Courage*—the bridge preparing you for the antidote.**

~ Chapter 2 ~
Coercion versus Brainwashing

I'm a survivor of domestic abuse. … It turned out everything my husband continually told me about myself and what I was capable of was completely wrong.

~ Angela ~ Survivor of Domestic Abuse ~

There's a significant and very important **difference between brainwashing and coercion**.

While **coercion is a subset of brainwashing; brainwashing is not a subset of coercion**. But both are about exercising power over another person to get them to do something that **they do not want to do**.

Now you might say, as many people do, that if they don't want to do something then they should just say no. And if you're one of those people, you are both extremely naïve and very arrogant and ignorant of what real life can be like. If only life was that easy, as I discussed in Chapters 1 and 2 of my book ***Brainwashed***.

So let's take a brief look at these two concepts one at a time: brainwashing and then coercion.

BRAINWASHING is a far deeper more subtle, and prolonged form of abuse than coercion. The beliefs the perpetrator is slowly embedding into their victim's mind, are done primarily through **subtle repetition**, often known as **grooming**. And because this is normally happening at a **non-conscious level**, most victims of brainwashing are not even consciously aware that **their values,**

beliefs, and indeed character are slowly being eroded away and changed.

This is clearly demonstrated in some of the early chapters of *Brainwashed,* especially in relation to my mother's **repeated "comments"** to me as a child. For example: "You'll never survive on your own. **YOU MUST** have a husband to take care of you."

And people ask why I didn't leave my abusive husband much sooner than I did. **The human need to survive** is one of the greatest human motivators of all. And my mother had **brainwashed** me to non-consciously believe that I'd never survive without a husband to take care of me.

Another doozie from my mother was: "If you want to play with your brother, you **MUST** play by **HIS** rules."

So to survive in life, I grew up believing that, in essence, I needed to (a) stay with my abusive husband. And what's more, (b) I MUST play by HIS rules.

And I'm certainly not Robinson Crusoe. Although definitely not as common today thank goodness, but there are so many women, especially women of more mature years, that I just KNOW will be able to relate to that sort of psychologically abusive, **negative brainwashing**.

In staying with my abusive husband and "following **HIS** rules" was I consciously doing something that I didn't want to do? No, not really. I might not have liked anything about it, but it was what I was brought up to do—"follow **HIS** rules." He was the man and so he was in control.

That's what disturbs me so much about the current very toxic teachings by the promoters of the so-called **"manosphere"**, who insist that women should still be subservient to a man.

So if you've read *Brainwashed,* you'll recall that even though I didn't like something, and as a child I thought that many things I experienced were **very "unfair"**, I still automatically believed that I was **acting of my own free will**. That this is just what life is all about. This is how someone is treated by a loved-one—by anyone for that matter.

But no, that's not necessarily the case at all.

COERCION, however, is about **exercising power, force, issuing threats, or violence, or even subtle psychological manipulation** to also get someone to act in a certain way, against their will. But it's normally done in **a very conscious and overt manner**. The victim knows exactly what's happening but due to the threats, or psychological manipulation, they agree to something that's totally against their wishes, values, and/or beliefs.

The table[2] on the next page highlights why confusing coercion with brainwashing leads to dangerous misunderstandings.

Some Real Life Examples of Coercion

As you'll see from the many different examples that follow, coercion can be successfully perpetrated in many different ways, sexually and non-sexually, against, and by, many different types of people. And that's why in Australia, the UK, and some states in the US such as Hawaii, at least **coercive control in relationships is a CRIMINAL offence**.

Now whether you're prepared to admit it or not, I have no doubt that at the lower levels of coercion, just to keep the peace, you've been **coerced** into doing something that you didn't really want to do.

Coercion happens to us all everyday, in expected and accepted ways and goes back thousands of years. Aristotle spoke of forms of coercion in the ***Nicomachean Ethics*** some 2300 years ago. When parents discipline their children, it's really another form of coercion. The child doesn't want to go to bed, but the parent will force the child to obey with the threat of withdrawing

Internet or computer privileges. And we have State sanctioned, or legal coercion. For example, we're forced to obey the laws of the land including road rules, with the **threat** of legal prosecution if we don't. It's all part of living in a functioning, ethical society.

Comparison of Coercion versus Brainwashing

Feature	Coercion	Brainwashing
Main Goal	Immediate Compliance: Forcing someone to *act* in a certain way, against their will, via various forms of threat, including removing freedom and independence	Conversion: Rewiring the victim's brain to *believe or think* a certain way often with long term outcomes.
Duration	Temporary: Once the threat is removed actions and beliefs go back to prior state	Long Term: Aims for deep, systematic changes in victims values, beliefs, character & even identity
Methods of Influence	External: Uses immediate fear, physical force, violence, short-term psychological manipulation, intimidation, or explicit threats	Internal: Uses subtle repetition of beliefs to be adopted, long-term psychological manipulation, grooming, all to erode critical thinking and change beliefs, values, and at times identity
Awareness	Conscious: The victim usually knows that they are being forced or manipulated to do something they do NOT want to do.	Non-Conscious: The victim will normally believe they are acting of their own free will, even though these actions might make them feel uncomfortable.
General Impacts	There's a great deal of overlap in the general impacts of coercion, brainwashing, and overall psychological abuse, and will differ with each person, but can often include fear, anxiety, confusion, guilt, shame, loss of true identity, powerlessness, depression, constant worry, disrupted sleep patterns, nightmares, and physical symptoms like headaches, fatigue, and muscle tension. Plus various cognitive difficulties, social and behavioural changes, impact on relationships, and lack of trust. And frequently, PTSD, self-harm, suicidal ideation, and suicide.	

But all too often illegal and most definitely **unethical coercion is common in the sales industry** with what's generally referred to as the "hard sell".

I clearly recall in the early days of Internet Marketing, 15 or 20 years ago, there were far more people promoting a product on the basis that you'll be the richest person around if you just purchase whatever it was they were selling. However, you were a no-hoper whose life would be worthless, or worse, if you didn't agree with what they were saying.

And give some thought to the millions of bullies in executive corporate positions who bully, **in other words coerce**, their staff to do their bidding. And for that matter, the leaders of countries who are no more than **bullies unethically coercing their constituents** to act in certain ways. And many of those countries call themselves "democracies".

Then for that matter, we have the leaders of sovereign states, **attempting to coerce the leaders of other sovereign states** to act in a certain way, under the threat of sanctions, or even attack. Frequently, these are offences under International Law—but it still happens, and it's coercion.

It's not uncommon for a woman to threaten self-harm if her "life-partner" says he plans to leave her. Or if she finds out that he's having an affair with another woman. Again, coercion at hand—if you leave me or continue the affair I'll self-harm, or maybe even kill myself.

And of course, we often see on TV depictions of the: ***give me the money or I'll kill you*** scenario—blackmail scenarios. Both of which are **forms of extreme coercion**—an extreme threat is made to get someone to doing something that they just don't want to do.

But it's in our **more intimate relationships** that we'll see, hear, and read of the most common forms of **criminal coercion**. This is currently clearly seen in the **Epstein Files** that I'll get back to shortly.

And all forms of negative coercion will have negative impacts.

Following are three totally different, but very common, **examples of coercion** that occur in family relationships. And I'll keep this review very brief because you can always get the details in ***Brainwashed*** if you'd like.

My Mother Coercing Dad into Selling Our Farm

When I was about 4 years of age, my Dad sold his business and fulfilled his life-long dream of buying a farm, a few hours south of Sydney.

But while Dad and I loved living on the farm, my sister, Dalla, who was 12 ½ years older than I was, and my brother, Rowley, 8 years my senior, hated being there. So both of them ended up moving back to Sydney and lived with our Grandmother. This left just me and my mother and father living on our wonderful farm, on the Southern Highlands, of New South Wales.

Now you might have heard the old saying "Happy Wife: Happy Life". In other words, if a man keeps his wife happy, there'll be a lot more harmony and happiness in the home.

Although, I can't really imagine my Dad necessary adhering to that saying. But I do know that he never wanted to leave the farm that he loved so much and had waited so long to acquire. Yet my mother couldn't get out of there quick enough. Maybe she threatened to leave him and join my sister and brother in Sydney if he didn't sell the farm. I don't know.

But Dad agreeing to sell his beloved farm to keep my mother happy, is one **very common form of coercion in a relationship**.

And the impact?

Following our move back to Sydney, Dad suffered severe (undiagnosed) clinical depression. A condition that was not understood in those days, back in 1966. But to me, today, it's very clear. He also suffered many of the general symptoms that I mentioned in the table above. Further, he went from being a light, social drinker, to consuming two bottles of rum and smoking 120 cigarettes **each and every day**. He was dead within about 7 years, at the age of 65.

People used to say to him: "You'll kill yourself if you keep drinking and smoking as you're doing."

To which he'd reply: "I'd prefer to be dead than give up the drink and smokes".

Rowley's coercion of my mother

When Dad did die he left my mother a great number of investment properties, so she'd have a very comfortable lifestyle for the rest of her life. Dad told us that he'd be doing that, on the verbal condition that on her death, my mother would leave all the property to my brother Rowley and me.

But Rowley started up a business of his own, and whilst he was a great salesman, he was a hopeless businessman. His answer was to continually **coerce** my mother into selling all the properties that Dad had left her, one-by-one, and handing the proceeds over to him. **Elder Abuse, via coercion, in the extreme.**

And the impact?

As I talk about in Chapter 9, ahead, "The Courage to Rise When No One Claps", at the age of 20, I lost my job, all of my family and family friends trying to prevent my brother's abuse of my mother. It was, without a doubt, **THE** most traumatic experience of my life. And I've been through some rippers over the years.

I also lost my share of my father's inheritance—a great many millions of dollars. And my mother ended up living her life out in a government provided bed-sitting room, existing on social welfare payments. Not at all what Dad had intended for her.

Josh "Coercing" Me into Taking Care of HIS Parents

Sadly, versions of the last two examples of coercion are relatively common in many families. The first example with my father eventually giving in to his wife to make her happy. And the second, with my brother, who had the ability to sell ice to the Inuit peoples, talking my mother into doing what he wanted her to do—sell all her properties and give him all the money.

And while this next example still involves a family context, it's significantly different in as much as it's based on **extreme psychological manipulation**—yet like the previous two examples, it was still at a conscious level, unlike a brainwashing event.

As a result, it's something to keep in mind, because while it's not as common as the first two examples of coercion, I'm not alone in what I experienced. Variations of how I let myself be **coerced as a result of psychological manipulation** are happening, especially to women, everyday, because **this is exactly how conmen work**. Even "conmen" that you might be married to.

As is often said, and it's so very true: …

Coercion is the abuse no one sees

until it's too late.

While the following story is, again, just a very brief overview, it is detailed, in Chapter 18 of ***Brainwashed*** ~ Déjà vu "All Over Again", including the dialogue of how it all went down.

There are six background points to keep in mind. They are:

1. As a child, my mother had brainwashed me into believing that I'd never survive, as an adult, unless I had a husband to take care of me. A belief commonly held by women my age.

2. Just as I had to abide by my brother's rules if I wanted to play with him, so too, non-consciously, that same brainwashing had me believing that I had to abide by my husband's rules. Another great falsehood, except for supporters of the manosphere. And that's why **the "manosphere" teaching are so very dangerous.**

3. Like my brother, former husband, Josh, was totally obsessed with the idea of making money, and had no moral compass whatsoever.

4. The very good-looking and charismatic Josh [aren't they all] spent his life working on one money making scheme after another. These were usually to do with buying and selling things: property but especially unique cars. But that also entailed getting mixed up with men who were just as money-focused and just as morally bankrupt as he was.

5. You'll recall the previous example of my brother coercing my mother into handing over to him all her money and properties, ultimately leaving her living in government housing; and me without any family, friends, or money. Just a very bad reputation concocted by my brother to hide his failures. And I give a few more details about that side of the story in Chapter 9, ahead.

6. Without a doubt, that was the most traumatic time of my life, and so yes, I'd naturally shared all the details with Josh.

Long story short, never one to miss an opportunity, former husband Josh, decided to do the same thing to his elderly parents, as Rowley had done to my mother.

Unbeknown to me, **Josh coerced his parents** into a 100% mortgage of their family home and giving him the money.

His "Method of Influence" in getting them to comply was twofold. First there was the promise of reaping great financial rewards from Josh's anticipated windfall investment gains.

And second, and I'm sure he played this one like Babe Ruth played baseball, he explained to them how much it would help their only child [Josh] achieve the financial greatness he'd coveted all his life.

I first heard about all of this after Josh came to me, explaining what he'd done to his parents, hence the ***Brainwashed*** chapter title, "Déjà vu, All Over Again" [thank you Yogi Berra[3], as opposed to Yogi Bear].

He continued to explain to me that his great money making scheme went pear shaped and he'd lost all the money his parents had loaned him. And his elderly parents were on the verge of losing their home, and ending-up out on the street, as had happened to my mother. ["Déjà vu, All Over Again"].

Knowing how traumatically I'd been affected by my brothers actions, Josh, the **master of psychological manipulation**, used every ploy in an attempt **to coerce me** into working, in essence, 6 or 7 days a week, using my inherent expertise to pay off **HIS** parents mortgage.

He played it out slowly, skilfully, patiently, and brilliantly, over a number of days, until I'd become putty in his hands. Ultimately, I agreed to "play by his rules", as my mother had taught me to do, and work as hard as I could for as long as it took to take care of **HIS** parents.

Me, taking care of **HIS** parents, became my major, and indeed only, purpose in life. And in ***Brainwashed,*** there are also a few twists in story as you go along.

And the reason that I share this story with you at this time is that coercion, through a form of **psychological manipulation** can have extremely long-term traumatic effects. Unlike some forms of coercion involving threats of harm or violence, what Josh did to me was to **"threaten" my very identity**—the person I believed I was—if I didn't comply with his wishes.

Briefly, his method was to take me back to what my mother went through in losing everything to Rowley—again, the most traumatic time of my life to that point.

In that very vulnerable state, he manipulated the conversation, and in so doing, manipulated me, to the point of having me agree that I had not helped my mother sufficiently to prevent her demise. And now, I was saying no to all his ideas of how I could help his parents.

So what sort of a perverted person was I to keep on seeing elderly people lose their homes. I should have done more to help my mother, and now when I have the opportunity to really help some people [his parents] I keep refusing. What sort of a shocking person was I?

By then, I had no family or friends to talk to about what he was doing, saying, and wanting me to do for him. And he'd been "brainwashing" me into believing that I was just "damaged goods", a total "no-hoper", due to all I'd been through as a child and then with my mother and brother only a few years before.

"After all, you must be a no-hoper", he'd continue: "If your own mother and brother want nothing to do with you".

And to prove what a shocking person I was, I was now refusing his plea for me to prevent his parents from ending up like my mother, in government housing, when I definitely had the ability to help them.

On and on and on it went, continually wearing me down. Day after day, after day, after day.

With that sort of on-going psychological manipulation, **he did destroy my very identity**—the essence of who I really was, the essence of who I believed I was. And with no one to talk with to convince me he was wrong, no one to believe other than Josh himself, and so **no one to trust, ESPECIALLY, not even myself**. I could no longer keep saying no, I will not do as you ask.

That sort of **psychological manipulation** is the cruellest, most subtle, and most divisive form of coercion one can experience. As I said above, it's "the abuse no sees until it's too late". But again, it's happening, especially to women, everyday.

So if you recognise any of those tactics, and all too many people who read this book will, run to the nearest professional for the help that's now available these days.

As the German sociologist, Max Weber said: Manipulation is the dark side of charisma.

~ Chapter 3 ~
Coercive Control and Sexual Coercion

Manipulation is the dark side of charisma.

~ Max Weber ~

Coercion explains what the headlines still get wrong.

In a similar vein to what I've already mentioned, "coercive control" is the term generally used when one partner in a relationship **attempts to control** the other partner, as Josh did to me. This is done through a pattern of controlling and manipulative behaviours, with all sorts of subtle and not so subtle threats for not agreeing with the perpetrator's wishes.

It's normally about making someone do things that will take away their dignity, self-respect, or identity; or just make them feel ashamed or even stupid. These acts might be of a sexual nature, but not necessarily. And while it's normally about one partner in a relationship attempting to control the other partner, again, it can also occur outside of an intimate life-partner relationship, as is the case with the **Epstein victims.**

So a word of warning, if you're experiencing any of the following[4], it's likely that your "partner" is attempting to "coercively control" you. These are just a sample of common coercive behaviours in intimate life-partner relationships. My former, and toxic husband, Josh, certainly used more than half of the following tactics on me on a regular basis.

- Isolating you from family and friends.
- Monitor your activity throughout the day.
- Denying you freedom and autonomy such as restricting your access to transportation, stalking you, or monitoring you via your phone.
- Gaslighting—Your partner will lie and manipulate the truth **so that you doubt your own truth, experience, and sanity**.
- Love Bombing with excessive or over-the-top gifts, compliments, and affection to manipulate or trap you.
- Name-calling and severe criticism.
- Limiting access to money and controlling finances.
- Turning your children against you.
- Controlling aspects of your health and your body by controlling how much you eat, sleep, exercise, or monitoring your weight or body shape.
- Making demands about the number of times you engage in sex and the kinds of activities you perform.
- Threatening your children or pets as an extreme form of intimidation.

If you're experiencing any of those behaviours, again please run, don't walk, to a professional for advice.

Impacts of Coercion in Intimate Life-Partner Relationships

A report[5] from "The NSW [New South Wales] Domestic Violence Death Review Team found about 97% of intimate partner domestic violence homicides in the Australian state of

NSW between 2000 and 2022 were preceded by the perpetrator using **emotional and psychological abuse as a form of coercive control towards the victim"**.

So again, NOT all coercive control led to homicide. But 97% of homicides were **preceded by coercive control**.

And in about 27% of these intimate partner homicides, there was no known history of physical violence before the victim was killed.

It's no wonder that **Coercive Control is a criminal offence** in some insightful and politically progressive countries.

But what about sexual coercion?

Sexual Coercion

Studies show that, at least, **1 in 3 women and 1 in 10 men** will experience some form of sexual coercion in their life. And I say "at least" because all forms of psychological abuse, of which sexual coercion is but one, are known to be very poorly reported due to fear, shame, embarrassment, or just "what's the point, no one will believe me", or "it was really all my fault", and the list of reasons continues.

Unlike coercive control which need not be sexual in nature, **sexual coercion** is always related in someway to sex, and like coercive control it can also occur inside or outside of an intimate partner relationship.

The Jeffrey Epstein case is a prime example of sexual coercion where no prior intimate relationship existed, as are most of the **#MeToo cases** that we began to hear about in 2017.

Sexual coercion can include a range of, and or combination of, activities including grooming, love bombing, badgering, guilting, and psychological manipulation. **All sexual coercion is both psychological abuse and sexual abuse.**

But, if as a result of this abuse and these threats, you give in and agree to the sex act, no matter how much you don't want to do it, the sex act itself is generally not considered a crime, unless you're under the age of legal consent. After all, once you agree then the act is mutual consent between consenting adults. However, it's **the initial coercion could well be a criminal offence** – albeit not always easy to prove.

While sexual coercion can occur on a continuum from low to high level approaches, research has found that **women who experience any form of sexual coercion** are more likely to experience self-blame and criticism, depression, anger, and even lower sexual desire and satisfaction, and frequently post-traumatic stress[6].

For most people, higher levels of coercion can be **a very traumatic experience.**

~ Chapter 4 ~
The Abuse that Leaves No Bruises *Can Still Kill*

Traumatic experiences leave a deep wound not only emotionally in the mind, but also physically in the brain, and can be fatal.

~ Dr. Bill Nash ~

Recently, I heard a very high profile man being interviewed about his recent divorce. The divorce was a surprise to everyone, especially the man himself. But it was a surprise to the general public too because he'd been married for about 30 years and they seemed like the perfect couple.

The interviewer asked if there had been any sexual infidelity, or abuse in the marriage. Quickly and very sincerely the man said "absolutely not—there was no infidelity from either one of us". He went on to say that there was no way that he would have physically or sexually abused his beautiful (now former) wife, whom he clearly loved dearly.

But **then the drop-the-mic moment came**. As a throwaway line he casually added: I was certainly very mentally and emotionally [or psychologically] abusive towards her.

"What do you mean?" The interviewer questioned in amazement.

"Oh well I was always yelling at her, and arguing with her, and chewing her out for not doing things the way I thought they should be done. So she left me".

"So she left me," he said. What a surprise!

I could hardly believe what I was hearing.

His inference was: it's **NEVER OK** to be physically or sexually abusive. And I agree 100% with that.

But getting angry and yelling and being psychologically abusive is just one of those things???

NO IT'S NOT!!!

It's Coercive Control 101

And again, that's why Coercive Control is a criminal offence in progressive societies including the US state of Hawaii, Australia, and the UK.

Indeed **anger** is often described as **the most moralistic emotion of all.**

Why?

Because when we get angry, we always believe that we're totally justified in getting angry. ***I am always right,*** and ***they are always wrong***. "Gosh, if the other person hadn't done/said the wrong thing, OR had done what I wanted them to have done, I wouldn't get angry would I?"

What a childish view that is.

But I have to say that more often than not there are two sides to every issue, whether that's a one-to-one personal relationship issue, a business issue, a community dispute, or even a global dispute.

When I worked with the Department of Justice as a sessional mediator/conciliator[7], even if I went into a session with my case notes indicating there could only be one side to a particular case, by the time I'd heard both sides, both had a position that was at least worth considering and definitely important to discuss.

As I explained in my Book 3 ~ *Conscious Self-Discovery,* if you dig beneath, what's known as, the "justification mechanisms", clearly a moralistic "I'm right" attitude is also due to **excessive negative ego**. And if an angry person is prepared to dig even more deeply, **past the moral outrage,** and **past the negative ego**, and into their **self-awareness**, they'll find **at the source of all the anger they have an underpinning fear** that one of their basic human needs is being threatened. And usually that fear has no foundation whatsoever.

How I would have loved to have had a long talk with that recently divorced man. A high profile man with a deep understanding of what was going on regarding psychological abuse and coercion, could well **help to change our world**.

And yet, despite his intelligence, he was just one more person who **had no idea what coercion is all about, and the trauma the victim can suffer as a result.** And worse still, he had **no understanding of the physical, literal, brain damage that trauma** can do to someone.

In *Brainwashed,* I share the story of **my only sister, Dalla, who took her own life** when she was 29. Like the high profile man above, her husband would never have physically or sexually hurt her. But like the high profile man above, in his own way, he too was very emotionally abusive—**psychologically abusive**.

Dalla died on February 15th, 1967, at a time when, culturally, women were far more reluctant than they are today, to leave an abusive marriage. But **leave the marriage she still did** in the only way she could think of at that time—**by killing herself**.

The real abuse isn't violence—**it's overpowering coercion** that has the potential to rewire the mind and damage the brain. **If**

you don't understand coercion, you just don't understand abuse.

It's true that everyone will react differently to a traumatic event. But just because many of Epstein's victim/survivors were OVER the age of consent, it doesn't mean that they were any less traumatised than were the under-aged girls—some even more so, for different reasons.

Not only does trauma lead to **a loss of self-compassion**, and so **a lot of self-blame**, but as you can read in *Brainwashed,* **trauma can have a life-time impact**.

As I've now said a number of times, trauma is not just about emotional/psychological upset. **Trauma actually causes physical damage to the brain.**

Sure, like any wound, over time the effects of that physical brain damage will gradually subside, especially with professional help. But that damage **will NEVER disappear** and as happened with Virginia Giuffre, years after her encounters with Jeffrey Epstein, the trauma was more than she could continue to live with, and so in April 2025, **she took her own life**.

And, Virginia Giuffre was the author of the book *Nobody's Girl,* about being sex-trafficked by Epstein to the former Prince Andrew amongst many others.

So if you happen to be one of Epstein's perverted male playmates and you're reading this book, and I do hope you are, know that your actions formed part of a chain of harm that contributed to **the unbearable trauma Virginia carried**, or whomever you victimised, carries.

As Lieutenant General Romeo Dallaire (ret.), who was the commander of the United Nations peacekeepers during the 1994 Rwandan genocide explained: **PTSD (Post Traumatic Stress Disorder) is potentially fatal.**

He said:

> People die of this [PTSD] injury. It might not be next week, but it can be at any time. Some noise; some

argument; some scenario could trigger a response that is uncontrollable and terminal.

And **that's exactly what happened with Virginia Giuffre**, and no doubt a great many other victims, not only of Epstein, but of similar contemptable, immoral excuses for men.

However, as I write in my Book 3 ~ ***Conscious Self-Discovery***, in Chapter 4 ~ "Diving Deeply", Megan Laslocky[8] suggests five key points that can help overcome an insecure life. And while those keys were specifically written for people with a negative childhood, they still apply to most forms of trauma-based brain damage. They include:

- **Get to know and understand what's going on for yourself at any time.**
- **Find a great therapist with expertise in PTSD**
- **If possible, seek out an understanding life-partner, although this can be a real tricky one for victim/survivors,** as I've discussed in other books.
- The most important one of all: **Practice opening up and talking about your feelings**, past, present, and future. And if you can't initially bring yourself to talk to your partner, or a confidant, or therapist, talk to your pillow or a teddy bear for practice. And yes, I'm serious about the teddy bear.

  And in case you're wondering, my special bear's name is Mr Edward T. Bear 😊.

  As I always say: **"You'll never get it out of your head unless you get it out of your head".** In other words, when the time is right for you, you've got to talk about it, to someone. See ***Brainwashed***, Chapter 27 ~ Post Traumatic Stress Disorder

  On this last very important point, I strongly recommend that you start writing about your past and your feelings in a Journal, if you don't already do so. Appendix A of Book 3 ~ *Conscious Self-Discover*, is all about **"Keeping a Self-Awareness Journal"**.

But the good news is that the effects of trauma-based brain damage can virtually disappear if you're lucky enough to experience **genuine loving, compassionate, non-judgmental, understanding, relationships** in the future. Ideally, this will be with an intimate life-partner, but it can be with any good and caring person.

Recently, I heard an interview on the radio with a woman who called herself an **"Empathic Dentist[9]"**. She said that those who've been through a sexual assault or trauma, can feel extremely powerless when being treated at the dentist. Afterall, you're sitting with your mouth open and all sorts of things going on in there, over which you have **NO CONTROL**. A lack of control is always key.

She went on to rightly say that victim/survivors of trauma need compassionate, non-judgemental, respectful relationships—all forms of relationships—with the understanding and acceptance that **what's happened to them is not their fault**.

What a wonderful woman.

Her "loving" empathy-based dentistry is changing people's lives.

You don't get over trauma—

you heal through love and kindness.

~ Chapter 5 ~
2017 and #MeToo

Every survivor deserves a space where they feel safe to share their experience. …

~ Letters to Pinterest Readers
Brittany, CC, and Tori ~

Sexual coercion in the extreme, and its long term traumatic after effects, could be seen world-wide, in 2017 with the exposure of what became known as #MeToo.

As I explained in my Book 7 ~ ***Conscious Feminine ENERGY***, the #MeToo hashtag was set up on Twitter, now X, in 2006 by Tarana Burke, the founder of a non-profit organisation that helps survivors of sexual violence.

However, it really made its presence felt on October 3rd, 2017, after ***The New York Times*** published the story detailing allegations of decades of sexual abuse perpetrated by the American film producer, Harvey Weinstein. It was then that the hashtag came to life.

The bottom line is that Weinstein would invite young women to his hotel suite to discuss their future film career. As many people fail to understand, this is not an uncommon practice, and it should be quite innocuous.

However, **Weinstein would then sexually coerce** the women with **the threat** of: Have sex with me and I'll help your movie career unfold. **No sex, no movie career**.

Within 48 hours the story led to over a million people Tweeting (now Xing???) on the **#MeToo hashtag** that "yes", they too had experienced something similar in their particular workplace. And it was happening in all workplaces, not just the entertainment industry.

The patterns of behaviour are always the same—grooming and coercion 101.

Within a week, versions of #MeToo in various languages had spread to eighty-five countries in all corners of the globe. Teams of journalists all over the world were starting to investigate similar allegations from thousands of women, about possible long-term perpetrators of inappropriate behaviour in their own specific country. Some of these allegations went back as far as seventy-five years in one particular case.

And I too added my name to the #MeToo tweet, having experienced a #MeToo incident on two separate occasions in years gone by.

Most importantly, it was my first #MeToo experience that led me to realise what was happening some years later when it happened for a second time. Both were very negative and distressing experiences. Both for very different reasons.

And so for the same reasons as I originally wrote ***Brainwashed***, just as my lived-experiences taught me more about life than any PhD could ever have done, I share these following two experiences for a number of reasons.

- If you are a victim/survivor, to let you know you're not alone.
- With the hope that my lived-experiences might be of help to each and every person who reads this book, whether they're a victim/survivor or not—or even a perpetrator.

  If you're one of the lucky few who've escaped these situations, you'll better understand what others have been through. And I guarantee that you'll know more people than you currently realise, who've **experienced some form of psychological abuse**.

- And to let you know that in the final chapter ahead, Chapter 9, I speak directly to a range of potential readers of this book, from victim/survivors, perpetrators, legislators, through to Anti-Violence Activists, and either explain a few key points, or **ask "WHY do you really do it?", as with the case of perpetrators**.

But I must add, that what my PhD **has** done is to give me the skills to write this book, and all my other books and deeply and competently analyse each and every situation in a multi-perspective manner, as my mediator/conciliator work also taught me to do.

Yes, there can even be another side to unconscionable perpetrators. Not the least of which is that they need urgent professional help.

My 1st #MeToo Experience

I first began to appear regularly on television around 1959, on the Sydney kid's show the "Channel 9-Pins". And then in the early 1980s, I began to do a lot of TV commercials, was a panellist on many live TV panel shows, and ended up as the **co-anchor of Good Morning Brisbane.**

After about a month on Good Morning Brisbane, the Executive Producer invited me to dinner to meet, a good friend of his and see his friend's show. This "good friend" was a very high profile entertainer from the UK who was touring Australia, appearing at all the top night spots.

Not only was I flattered that the producer had invited me to join him, but I was as excited as all heck at the thought of meeting his "good friend"—a real household name at the time.

The dinner was wonderful. The show was great, as expected. And after the show the entertainer came to our table and began a brief catch-up chat with his good mate—my producer. To continue their conversation, without people coming up for autographs [no selfies in those days] the entertainer invited us upstairs to his suite.

He too had worked in the UK on a similar show to Good Morning Brisbane, so I had a million questions I wanted to both "subtly", "casually", and not so subtly ask him. But after about 20 minutes, or so, the entertainer received a phone call.

Long story short, the entertainer said he wouldn't be able to "entertain" us any longer. He had another "friend" waiting for him in the room down the hall and he wouldn't be back.

But he invited my producer to continue our conversation in his very luxurious suite, complete with all the free and delicious food and drink that the hotel had provided.

My producer saw the entertainer to the door, and they had a brief chat, and when the producer returned, what a "production" he'd arranged.

I was in my early 30s, so I guess I should have known better. But I'd had no reason not to trust him. Afterall, he was the man who'd given me this great opportunity to co-host a major daily capital city TV show.

And so when he excused himself to go to the bathroom, and returned wearing **NOTHING** but a loosely tied bathrobe, I knew what **I was really there for**.

I often think how I'd love to be in that situation today, with my understanding of the world and some of the people in it. **I'd have gleefully destroyed the bastard in some way—so good on you Virginia**.

But it was a different time and a different world back then.

I had no idea what to do. I kept saying to myself, **it's your own fault**. **You've** put yourself in this room with him. **YOU SHOULD** have run out of the room when the entertainer left. **But YOU didn't. YOU'VE got no one to blame but yourself.**

Although I was definitely NOT to blame at all.

But heck, I kept thinking that due to my past marriages it wasn't going to be my first rodeo. Plus, after my time with Josh, I kept reliving his words that I was just **"damaged goods"— "a real no-hoper"**. So who was I to complain about anything?

The "damaged goods" label is a very common one for victim/survivors of sexual abuse, especially as children.

And when it came to the producer, I certainly didn't want to do anything sexual with him and I made it clear that it was not what I wanted. Sure, I always found him interesting to talk with and so I'd have been happy to continue with a casual conversation—but not this.

Goodness, I found him as sexual attractive as a house brick. However, even far more than that, I was so thoroughly repulsed and disgusted by what was clearly such a depraved duplicitous set-up. **The seeming assumption that that's all I was there for made me feel so dirty.**

Yet, he was the man with my TV career in his hands.

But still, the words: "It's all your own fault" kept ringing in my head. As did: "So you do know what you have to do now. Just get on with it and pretend it isn't happening to you."

Just as the well-know idiom from the early 20th century was used to induce a form of dissociation in such circumstances: "Just lie back and think of England".

So that's what I did. And I hated myself for doing it, and I still hate myself, to this very day, for it all.

Later he drove me home. It was a Friday night and not only did I spent the entire weekend curled up in a greatly distressed foetal state in bed. But on Monday morning, I continued to co-host the TV show as if nothing had happened.

However, that following week the producer came back wanting "seconds". I came up with some excuse about being busy that night. But due to his on-going persistence, I ran out of excuses. It was then that I realised that far from my future TV career being in his hands, my future TV career was obviously between his legs. And so I took the only way out that I could think of. **I resigned.**

On the one hand, as my TV career was over I should have gone to the police. What else could I lose? But in those days, even the police would not have believed that there was anything wrong with something like that.

In ***Brainwashed,*** I talk about being abducted, restrained, and raped by a Catholic Priest when I was 23. About 25 years later, when I was working as a talk-back radio broadcaster, the "off-the-record" story of the rape was written up in the city's newspaper, with a banner headline on the front page. And I was portrayed as having made it all up. It was the late 1980s, and the inference was "Gosh a priest would never do anything like that". It took another 10 or so years before the world discovered that **YES, a Catholic Priest would indeed do that sort of thing**.

So now, with the producer, here I'd once again put myself in a position of **a lack of control.** And a lack of control was one of the may reasons that I escaped from Josh when I did.

But back then, never once did I **blame** the producer for any of his actions. I continued to think he was a contemptible, perverted, sexual cretin. But I didn't **blame** him.

Instead, just as the research continually shows, while **I hated what had happened, I hated *MYSELF* even more—I blamed myself**. I kept saying to myself, "**how could you have let it happen**?" **"How could you have been so stupid?"**

Today, the producer's actions **were in essence rape**. Especially considering the dinner, the show, meeting his high profile entertainer mate who "suddenly had to leave the room", and the producer knowing the power he had over me due to his position as my producer. Those actions were **all sexual coercion—grooming 101** at its best. **All illegal activities**. But again, sexual coercion, and grooming, were unknown concepts back then.

Yet **even today**, in 2026, I've never been able to regard his actions as **the premeditated rape** that it was. **I still hold myself completely to blame for putting myself in that position.**

AND those sorts of character changing self-recriminations never leave you. **They are with you for life**. And they are very commonly held by victim/survivors of any sort of coercive control, not just sexual coercion.

So moving forward, I kept trying to convince myself of the old saying that: "Whatever happened to you in the past, doesn't define you."

Meanwhile for the perpetrator: he's had another successful score—***Yaaaaaaa***. Who cares about the injured party—the woman who would live with the event **for the rest of her life**.

But what it did do was prepare me in case it ever happened again—which it did.

My 2nd #MeToo Experience

As I keep saying, **the patterns of behaviour** are always the same.

So here goes.

I'd been working on radio for some years, moving from station to station as my profile and opportunities increased. But I still hadn't achieved the level of success I'd been striving for. Then, long story short, what appeared to be my "big break" came knocking.

Arguably, the most powerful radio executive in Australia invited me to discuss a golden opportunity to do a full-time Monday to Friday talk radio program in my favourite capital city, at my favourite time-slot. The executive was a lovely man that I'd met and spoken with on a number of occasions over the years.

But ask **any of the Epstein victim/survivors** and they'll all agree. These MEN don't ask if you'd like to have sex with them. There's just an expectation.

They all have the egocentric, narcissistic expectation that **of course you'd like to have sex with such a powerful, high profile man.** Or the egocentric, narcissistic expectation that you'd only be thinking one thing: Of course I'd love to have sex with you **if you can help me attain the successful career I so long for**". Isn't just the art of the deal???

I'm sure you'll recall the words, which went global, from one of Epstein's high profile, rich and powerful mates: "I don't even wait. And when you're a star, they let you do it. You can do anything.... Grab 'em by the ..... ." [10]

As was common and innocuous practice, the radio executive wanted to discuss the proposed deal away from the radio station. After all, he didn't want anyone to know he was talking with me, and have them put two and two together and correctly assume he was talking with me about a forthcoming radio station vacancy. Yes, a forthcoming vacancy, of which the current presenter knew nothing about—**also a very common yet NOT so innocuous occurrence in radio.**

As an example, one day someone I worked with went to the sandwich shop down the road from the radio station to buy her lunch. She presented a Monday to Friday on-air program. And while the shopkeeper was making her sandwiches he said to her: "So when are you leaving your show?" Perplexed, she replied: "I'm not leaving?"

The shop owner, who'd experienced this sort of thing before thought he should be up front with her, replied: "Oh yes you are"! He then went on to tell her what everyone seemed to know, but her. She was about to be fired.

So I had to meet the radio executive in the lounge area of the hotel he was staying at—he lived in another state. He then explained that because both of our faces were well known in town, that he'd arranged for dinner to be served in his hotel suite. That was also kinda common practice in that situation.

We entered his room and there in front of me was a beautiful big dining room table able to seat six, with just two places prepared.

So far so good.

Again, all was really very common practice for the sort of media discussion about to take place.

We ordered a beautiful "silver service" type dinner—something I'd always loved. Once served, the waiter left the room, leaving the dessert and coffee on the sideboard for us to take care of ourselves. As we consumed the most fabulous dinner, we spoke at length about the current status of the radio industry in Australia. He always had some fantastic stories to share.

The more the radio executive spoke with me, the more there was no doubt in my mind, that my long held radio dream was about to come to fruition, as he told me what he had in mind for me.

BUT, what he told me was only PART of what he had in mind for me.

With the dessert and coffee out of the way, he finally wanted to continue the "discussion" in greater comfort in the adjoining room, rather than continuing to sit on the upright dining room chairs.

And the adjoining room?

Why that was the bedroom.

My previous #MeToo experience came flooding back like Niagara Falls in the rainy season. As we stood up, I just made up some garbled, incoherent excuse and **literally ran out the door and into the hotel hallway,** leaving him standing there watching me in amazement.

The next day, I had a previously arranged open meeting with him and the station manager. This time it was at the radio station. I assumed that it was to discuss the details of my new dream job.

I arrived on time. But the executive kept me waiting for well over an hour. He finally appeared at the waiting room door and sternly just said: "After the way you treated me last night, you will never work anywhere in radio ever again." And he made sure that I didn't.

And who could I even complain too—everyone directly or indirectly reported to him?

It was after that encounter, that I began the next phase of my life as a fulltime university student.

Now it was one thing to lose my TV work, because I really was not disciplined enough to work on TV. **I didn't enjoy working on TV in the least**. And so I was kinda proud of myself for resigning from the job.

But **I was devastated to lose my radio work**. I loved it so much. I'd spent so many years getting to the stage I had. And I was helping so many of my listeners, in all sorts of wonderful ways.

Heck, a few years before, I'd even **won the top radio award for the best talk broadcaster on Australian radio.**

Now that was not as much for the way I sounded, but more for the way I helped my listeners. And this one man put an end to it all because he didn't get the sexual jollies he'd planned on getting the night before.

Such is the power of high-profile elites who don't get what they want in life.

Needless to say, over the years I've thought a great deal about both of those #MeToo events. For me, I ended up in those compromising situations **due to my insatiable thirst to learn as much as I can from everyone I have the opportunity to talk with**. I guess that's what helped make me an award-winning talk-radio broadcaster.

But goodness me, did I ever have a "learning-experience" from both of those #MeToo events.

On neither occasion, did the thought of sex ever even cross my mind before the event. By contrast, for both men clearly sex was the ONLY thought that not only crossed, but was also anchored, in their disgusting minds.

I certainly learned that you must always be aware of how you're potentially being manipulated. **I was just far too trusting**.

A rich and powerful man once insisted that **too many people ERRONEOUSLY think** that the rich and powerful are evil and that they just go after whatever THEY want.

And while I know that's not true for **ALL** the rich and powerful men out there, but as I talk about in Chapter 6, ahead, and also in my Book 8 ~ ***Conscious Leadership,*** **all too many rich and powerful men ARE definitely that way**.

As we're currently finding out with the release of more and **more of the Epstein Files**, if you get into trouble and have enough money you can buy the best legal defence team and move on unscathed—an option not available to the vulnerable in society, especially those with not much money.

The rich and powerful elite know, and want to know, other rich and powerful people. And that's understandable. Like attracts like.

But they all have the money and **the power that goes with that money**. And all too often, they use that money and power in highly unethical ways, **going after whatever they want** without even the slightest thought as to how innocent parties might be hurt in the process.

Then, as "playmates" together, more often than not they'll circle the wagons to protect each other no matter what horrific deeds they know have been going on.

And THAT'S what's evil about all too many of the rich and powerful who do that sort of thing.

And goodness me, has that ever been "exposed" [excuse the pun] as is happening with the Epstein Saga and the infamous Epstein Files.

~ Chapter 6 ~
The Epstein Files

Those who overcome their fears will truly be free.
~ Aristotle ~

The release of the Epstein Files is not merely a political event, nor simply a criminal matter. It's also **a moral stress test** for **modern democracies world-wide**.

When wealth, power, secrecy, and sexual exploitation intersect at the level of **the Epstein Saga**, we're no longer examining the actions of just one man. We're examining the **ethical foundations of entire systems—the legal system, political system, cultural system, and overall societal system.**

So this chapter is not just about the Epstein side-show or headlines. As with previous chapters, **it's about coercion**—how it operates, how it spreads, and how it protects itself.

And by mid-February 2026, social media was overflowing with comments that the Epstein Saga was **the biggest cover-up in American history**. Other comments include that it's **a crisis unequalled since WWII** or **even since the Civil War**. Such is the general publics' distress, no matter which political party you support.

Republican Congressman, Thomas Massie, commented that the Epstein cover-up was **worse than Watergate**[11].

The worst crimes always end, not due to the overt crime itself, but due to the attempted cover-up. Cover-ups rarely work in the long-term. Look at Al Capone. The authorities couldn't get him for murder, or bootlegging, or any of his other crimes. His comeuppance was due to the covering-up of his income: so tax evasion.

The current lack of transparency associated with the Epstein Files will, no doubt, ultimately have a very interesting conclusion.

So what are the Epstein Files?

The Epstein Files are a trove of documents; 300+ gigabytes of data, emails, photographs, and FBI reports detailing the criminal activities of the American financier and convicted "child" sex offender Jeffrey Epstein and his affiliates—his playmates.

A convergence of wealth, power, and moral exemption.

Many influential men that **Epstein "targeted"**, and so are mentioned in the Epstein Files, said no. Not interested in any part of you. And good for them.

But as is now appearing in the files, a great many men whose power insulated them from accountability, yet whose ego-centric sexual appetites eclipsed any moral restraint, **were also played by Epstein with the skills of Yehudi Menuhin playing a Stradivarius—Coercion 101**.

And they said yes please Jeffrey my dear friend—count me in and thank you so very much for including me as a friend of yours. Offering sex to these rich and powerful men was like offering candy to a child.

As Machiavelli said, "... he who seeks to deceive will always find someone who will allow himself to be deceived." And was Epstein ever one to deceive—anyone and everyone.

And while virtually all the attention on the Epstein Files has been related to the sexual side of Epstein's world, **there's**

another side that should be of almost, or even greater, concern that I'll get onto shortly.

But for now, with regard to Epstein and the Epstein Files, let's focus on **the coercive side of his sex-trafficking activities**.

Now I don't need to go into the details of these documents to recognise the emerging **sexually perverted patterns of behaviour** of Epstein and his equally sickening sexually perverted, "powerful", money-rich elite playmates. Men—including politicians, royalty, celebrities, corporate elites, no category is left out—who because of their power, money, and narcissistic ego, seemed to have believed that their status signalled immunity. And that they'd be untouchable.

And so far, most of these men in the United States appear to have remained untouched.

Surely you can't have 1000 to 2000 victims, many of whom have given explicit details of what they endured, 6 million pages of FBI and DOJ files, 2000 videos, and 180,000 images, and **yet NO convictions?** Come on now.

When allegations accumulate at scale without proportional accountability, **systemic institutional integrity must be questioned.** Again including legal systems, political systems, cultural systems and societal systems.

Sure, with the last tranche of files released on January 30th, 2026, a number of high profile names **have appeared**. But we were also told that there are many more names that are still in "hiding"—having been redacted.

These rich and powerful men, and on the odd occasion some of their culpable wives, must ALL be held to account for their actions in some way.

Initially, had the former Prince Andrew not had such a prior questionable reputation, I might ALMOST have felt sorry for him.

Why?

Because up until the last tranche of data, he was the only man to be so publicly outed, **and so publicly punished** for his involvement with Epstein.

What about the rest of them? *Ah but then!*

Yes, as you're probably aware, the US Department of Justice (DOJ) were compelled by law to release all Epstein documents by December 19th, 2025. But it kept releasing bits and pieces at a time, with much of the contents being redacted until the January 30th, 2026[12] tranche when the previously mentioned three million pages of documents were released, including 2000 videos and 180,000 images.

At that time, the U.S. Deputy Attorney General, Todd Blanche[13], announced to the world that the DOJ held yet another two and half million pages that **would NEVER be released** but "there was nothing he could do about that".

WHY NOT???

What about the legal requirement to release **all the files???**

This really does raise serious questions about procedural transparency.

And then the only redactions were to be anything that identified the victims. Instead, many of the victims' details were left **UNredacted**, while perpetrators details **WERE** redacted.

Again, over the years, victims reported to the FBI what had happened to them. Graphic and often horrific reports which now appear in this latest tranche of documents. But, **up until now**, those reports were seemingly ignored by the FBI.

So who is a victim meant to report to???

The failure of ethical reporting pathways is itself an example of a **systemic ethical crisis.**

In the late 1970s, I had a casual job working in an illegal casino in Sydney. Yet the "illegal" casino operated openly without any problems. Not only that, but the casino was frequented by all the rich, famous, and powerful members of Sydney's elite, plus politicians, the judiciary, and off-duty police.

How come???

Well at that time the most common catch-phrase around town was that Sydney had **"the best police force that money could buy"**. And goodness me, the rich and powerful had all the money required to **"buy" that police force in whatever way they desired**.

I'll leave you to come to your own conclusions with regard to the so-called US authorities and the Epstein Files. But it does beg **the coercion question**.

To what extent have all those behind the systemic ethical crises in the United States—the lack of transparency in all its many forms—been **coerced into acting that way**, and by whom?

Meanwhile, this drip feed of documents is significantly adding to the trauma already experienced by victim/survivors who want **EVERYTHING ALL** out in the open as soon as possible, and dealt with, so that they can get on with their lives.

Personally, after researchers began to discuss the shocking and sickening stories they we're discovering in those files released on January 30th, I had an extremely negative reaction. So much so that I was unable to work at all for several days. And this one chapter, with its associated research, has been one of the hardest pieces of writing I think I've ever done. It's taken so long to complete—days, and days, and days, and days .... .

Stories reportedly found in the newly released documents include all the obvious rapes of underaged girls and young women that we're hearing about. But there are also stories about the young girls who became pregnant as a result of their rape. And then the stories of what happened to those babies, if the pregnancy ever went full term. The files talk about the alleged deaths of some of these young girls resulting from rough sex. Claims of torture. As Epstein himself said in one email I saw: "I loved the torture video".

You can do your own research if you want to find out more. Go to the DOJ files yourself at https://www.justice.gov/epstein Or just do a Google or YouTube search for Epstein Files a few times, and those little algorithms will keep feeding you all the Epstein pop-ups you could ever want, **or not want,** to see.

While it's true that these days there are many fake AI reports on YouTube covering every topic imaginable. So watch out for those—don't be deceived. But there are many genuine "citizen journalists", and reputable podcasters and YouTubers who've been around a long while and whose reporting is normally credible.

After the Endnotes, I've included a URL Bibliography, listing a several pages of YouTube URLs from credible YouTubers, covering a wide range of Epstein related topics, including all those discussed throughout this chapter. Many of the videos have screen shots of actual emails and documents from the DOJ files.

BUT one further word of *WARNING*—some of the content in those videos is far from pleasant to hear about.

So **perpetrators, do remember** that while YOU were having YOUR sexual jollies at Epstein's "fun-parks", **trauma never leaves a victim/survivor**.

Trauma Never Leaves a Victim/Survivor

Sure we're able to lock it away in our non-conscious mind and continue with life as if nothing was wrong. But you'll recall the words of Lieutenant General Romeo Dallaire (ret.) in Chapter 4 above.

> People die of this [PTSD] injury. It might not be next week, but it can be at any time. Some noise; some argument; **some scenario could trigger a response that is uncontrollable** and terminal.

Epstein's playmates might have plenty of power and money, but **power and money without empathy is purely predation.**

Surely there's nothing more masculine that protecting young girls and women from sexual predators. And there's **nothing weaker or more vile and disgusting** than sexually preying on vulnerable young girls and women.

But The Elephant Emerges:

Epstein's ***COVERT*** Business Model?

Setting aside the depraved and debauched sexual side to the Epstein Files, which disgusts and angers me as I mentioned in passing at the start of this chapter.

But there's **another dark side that should be of great concern to everyone**. Something that also angers me greatly and frightens the heck out of me.

Out of the three million odd pages that were released on January 30th, an elephant began to emerge in the form of potentially two distinct business models. This is in answer to the main question so many people kept asking: Where did all Epstein's money and power come from?

For a long time, the dots have been scattered all over the place like the trail of breadcrumbs that Hansel and Gretel left in the forest. It's just a matter of attempting to connect all of those dots **before the birds REDACT all the breadcrumbs**.

For years it's been suggested that Epstein had some links to international organisations – groups like Mossad, Israel's national intelligence agency, and similar connections in Russia. And there were even rumours of a connection with a shadowy global cabal of extremely rich and powerful men who were attempting to "capture democracies". All pretty wild.

But as I'll demonstrate in a moment, if that WAS true, it would certainly answer the "where did Epstein's money come from" question, and so many other questions as well, about the whole Epstein Saga.

Now I'm not into conspiracy theories here. BUT I know enough about the world to always be, **at least**, open to the most seemingly unbelievable theories, until such time as I'm given **credible evidence of their falsehood,** which I'll just as happily accept. It's the evidence that I'll always chase and analyse.

So let me tell you about **a fascinating 28:13 minute documentary,** that I recently watched on the MSN website. The doco was put together by a YouTuber, who goes by the name of "Moon". And after watching that video, I too would want to remain anonymous if I'd produced the video.

After all, it's said that close to 30 people who were linked in some way to the Epstein Saga have now mysteriously or suddenly died – allegedly including Epstein himself.

And, give me whatever name you like, but I have no hesitation in saying that personally, from day one, I've **NEVER** believed that Epstein killed himself.

Then there are even those who believe Epstein is still alive currently relaxing on some secret island somewhere, laughing his head off at all that's going on in his name, at this time. Enjoying his new life as he watches the rich and powerful dominoes fall world-wide, nation-by-nation, as top diplomats and high profile elites are "exposed" in the saga. And as he, no doubt, wonders how long it will take before America experiences the same major collapse in his name as in other countries, like the UK.

Now when I wrote the first draft of this book my following comment at this point was: Suicide No way. But still alive? Now that really IS a bit of a stretch.

But with an open mind, I kept digging.

Since then, with all the evidence still emerging from the January 30th tranche of documents, the inconsistencies surrounding Epstein's death definitely need a lot greater independent scrutiny than they've currently received.

Now I could write pages and pages discussing the potential evidence that keeps coming to light, regarding these "inconsistencies". But I won't.

Instead, I'll just list a number of areas worth considering and let you make up your own mind as to Epstein's death, or not.

One of the most reported "inconsistencies" is that nothing adds up in his jail area around the time Epstein died. From lost surveillance tapes, to guards falling asleep, a discrepancy in the date on official documents about his death, guards forgetting to do their 30 minute checks on him, he was meant to have a cell mate—but didn't. Through to the implausibility of Epstein tearing up enough of his untearable bed linen to do the job[14].

But the real clangers are now associated with Epstein's autopsy. There's an image doing the rounds on social media, which I've seen, showing the ears and nose of the man who was allegedly autopsied as Jeffrey Epstein, versus those of the REAL Jeffrey Epstein. And if the images are real, the two images are quite different[15]. As yet, I've not seen any explanation for those differences, nor anyone saying they're fake. So who knows?

And ears are a bit like fingerprints. Virtually everyone has a unique ear shape. Not only that, but there were alleged unusual aspects to Epstein's genitalia, which has been discussed in a number of online newspapers and videos. But the man autopsied is alleged to have had quite "normal" genitalia.

And if all that's not enough, the forensic pathologist who conducted the autopsy signed off on the official report saying that the cause of death was "inconclusive". However, several days later, her superior changed the official "inclusive" verdict to suicide. In addition, top pathologist, Dr Michael Baden, with over 20,000 autopsies under his belt, also attended the autopsy. And he said the body was not consistent with a suicide.[16].

Now I'm not necessarily saying that all of that is 100% true. All I'm saying is that it adds to the many unanswered questions that keep coming to light about this saga and so warrants "some very serious scrutiny". Scrutiny that it's not receiving.

That brings us back to Republican Congressman, Thomas Massie's comment (from the start of this chapter), that the **Epstein Saga is a bigger cover-up than Watergate**.

And the only way any such cover-ups work is through **unethical, high-level, on-going** corruption based on **systemic coercion**.

But back to "Moon's" documentary.

There are social media posts offering many different potential real names for Moon. And except for his YouTube channel, there's hardly one positive comment about his work in the general social media, despite his 1.61 M followers. The most common complaint is not that what he says is wrong, but that he's a plagiarist.

And as a former academic I too HATE plagiarism, which is probably why I've just put together half a page talking about the source of the video link that I'm about to share with you. And maybe Moon, would do a lot better if they always gave a source for the fascinating information they use.

Having said that, this particular YouTube doco, titled "Jeffrey Epstein: How a Government Spy Blackmailed America" with the URL of https://tinyurl.com/Bk7a-coercion certainly kept my attention.

While I can't attest to the accuracy of everything said in the Moon documentary. But again if true, the doco answers many questions about the entire Epstein Saga. So in the rest of this chapter, if I refer to the broad allegations in the Moon doco supported by other relevant information in the Epstein Files themselves, I'll refer to them as **"Epstein's *COVERT* Business Model"**.

So, when it comes to "Epstein's COVERT Business Model" we should all be extremely concerned and vigilant should there be any truth in that side of the Epstein Saga.

However, I suggest that you check out the Moon video for yourself and make your own conclusions. But as they'd say on the TV show, MythBusters, it certainly is "Plausible".

Meanwhile anything further to do with Epstein's Covert Business Model, beyond passing comments below, and the above YouTube URL, is way beyond anything that I want to get involved with here, in this little book.

My sole concern is with the victims associated with **Epstein's *OVERT* Business Model**, and the victims of similar degenerate networks. And that's what I'll now focus on.

Speculating on the Dots in this Saga

Disclaimer—An Important Note

What follows, through to the end of this chapter, is purely speculation that I've made by joining the dots found in the Epstein Files and widely reported. There are some comments for which I have cited a specific source. However, just because I've referenced the sources of some of my comments, it doesn't mean that what the source is saying is necessarily a statement of proven fact either.

The Epstein Saga has a number of major dots or interacting components that are becoming more and more evident with the release of the latest tranche of files including—**sex, money, power, influence**, and **secrets.** Oh and **alleged blackmail** which just happens to also be **a form of high level coercion**.

Although everything to do with the Epstein Saga, at both the covert and the overt levels, seems to have a foundation of **coercion.**

But the genesis of the Epstein Saga is a bit like the chicken and the egg. Which came first?

What a great PhD research topic this will be in the not too distant future.

So let's take a look. And we'll start with the Sexual side of things, seeing as that's the main area the "overt" model focuses on.

After reading some of the unredacted files, Democratic Congressman, Jared Moskowitz of Florida,[17] said in an interview with CNN: that the Epstein Saga was a "Worldwide sex-trafficking network with people in other countries [including France, Russia, and Czechia] sourcing young children for Epstein." With Epstein's playmates being well aware of the paedophilia they were involved in, as evidenced by their receipt of many emails from Epstein. For example, one email said: "We're dropping the child off to you..."

Epstein's ***Overt*** Business Model—Starting with Sex:

So... Once Upon a Time ...

There are psychological profilers on YouTube who've analysed Epstein's obsessed predilection for massages: **coercive-sourced, sexual massages.** They say that Epstein's biggest problem is that he had a **"sexual massage addiction"**. But I totally disagree.

While I'm sure he enjoyed a massage: most people do. But I suggest that massages were just Epstein's shtick to **recruit and coerce** someone into **the sex he craved**, for a number of reasons.

Like my former husband, Josh, **Epstein was a sex addict**—as plain and simple as that. Not that any addiction is really "plain and simple", but I'm sure you know what I'm saying.

But he clearly was **not ONLY a sex addict**. Again, I suggest that he was also **addicted to the money** and **the power** and **the influence**, that that money attracted. Addictions, that so many people have. Again, including my former husband.

Indeed Josh was so addicted to money that he came up with **an ALMOST foolproof fast money scheme**. He took an insurance policy out on my life, and then attempted to drown me in a rip at a deserted beach.

So let's move on to the money, power, and influence dots for a moment, and permit me to **speculate** once again, on how those dots could well be connected, based on what has come out of the files so far.

Money, Power, Influence, and Secrets

WOW!!! What a quadrella that is!

This is where things move into a totally different realm and can't really be separated. This is where the dots are like the shining lights on the Las Vegas strip. Just as bright. Just as obvious. And now even being confirmed with the January 30th release of the 3 million pages of Epstein Files.

At some point in time, Epstein, a nobody, but a very charismatic nobody, got to know a number of powerful, rich, and influential individuals, one of whom was Ghislaine Maxwell. She had all the money and powerful influential contacts Epstein needed to develop what was indeed **a very strategic business plan**.

Knowing how important sex was **to him**, Epstein knew that there must be other men who felt the same.

Well whoop-de-doo no surprises there!

Their Secrets

Also, all rich and powerful and influential men will have secrets to keep, in some form. And if they didn't? With all his surveillance cameras in every room, it's believed by some that Epstein ensured that they ultimately would have secrets they'd want to keep.

So, Epstein set out to become besties with as many rich, powerful, and influential men as possible. Then in the course of a conversation by the pool, those same rich, powerful, and influential men, could probably have the irresistible urge to big note themselves by bragging to their special friend, the very charismatic Jeffrey Epstein, about some of their business, or political, or even national secrets. And those sorts of secrets are worth more than the spot price of gold on the highest day possible.

For example, ever since the release of the late Virginia Roberts Giuffre's book ***Nobody's Girl***, in October 2025, we've known about the former Prince Andrew's association with Epstein and his alleged sexual exploits with some of Epstein's girls.

But in what has been described as "more than just a crisis" yesterday, on Andrew Mountbatten-Windsor's 66th birthday, six unmarked police cars rolled up to Andrew's home and arrested him on "suspicion of misconduct in public office"—a very open "suspicion" that could include all sorts of things. He spent 11 hours in custody, was questioned, and then released.

However, what's now emerging is that, at this stage, the UK police are now investigating Andrew beginning with allegedly sharing confidential UK trade secrets and investment opportunities with Epstein[18].

Information that I suggest could be worth many millions to Epstein, either directly, or via his alleged **Covert Business Model** too.

It's been nearly 400 years since a senior member of the royal family has been arrested in such a manner and treated like any other common criminal.

It must be noted that Andrew still protests that he's done nothing wrong. But in a major departure from Royal tradition, King Charles has commented on the case, with Buckingham Palace announcing that "The King ... expressed his 'deepest concern'... and that he is ready to support the police and co-operate with the police.[19]".

WOW!!! For anyone who knows anything about royal protocol – **that is big stuff.**

Similarly, the BBC[20] online also reports that the UK "Metropolitan Police has launched a criminal investigation into [Lord Peter Mandelson] over allegations of misconduct in public office".

The Epstein files, contains emails in which Mandelson, the now former UK Labour minister and now former US ambassador, "likely sent market sensitive government information" to Epstein. Like Andrew Mountbatten-Windsor, these investigations have resulted in the loss of Mandelson's political connections, his job, and he's had to step down from the House of Lords.

Then numerous other reports[21] abound of alleged links that Epstein had with countries including France, Poland, Lithuania, Norway, Slovakia, and major links with Israel and Russia. These were mainly related to allegations of information or money transfers; which could be directly linked to both **Epstein's Overt as well as his alleged Covert Business Plans.**

And my question is this. If all of these countries are so concerned about links that the powerful and rich people in their specific countries had to Epstein, that they're all initiating major investigations into what's showing up in the Epstein Files, **why isn't the USA doing the same thing?**

Instead, in the USA, predators names are being redacted while victims' identities are being exposed.

Officials have said that these paper files of allegations of specific high profile men are all just "hearsay" and so not able to be used in court, or even be investigated.

Okay, so maybe the information is not able to be used in court at this stage. BUT surely that's why the reports MUST be investigated, to find court approved evidence.

Officials have said that they need an actual victim to come forward and testify in court. But setting aside the many nondisclosure agreements **the girls were coerced into signing**, these girls are afraid to speak up. Afraid for their very lives.

So what about the roughly 2000 videos, and 180,000 images that were released, and the others still to come? I'm sure that those videos aren't just showing Tom and Jerry cartoons. In fact I've seen some, and neither Tom nor Jerry appear at any time. There has to be some damming evidence there or Epstein would not have taken them or kept them.

So to sum all of that up.

Where did Epstein get all his money from?

Again speculation, by joining the dots from the Epstein Files and the numerous online reports.

Epstein coerced all his rich and powerful playmates to share their secrets with him. Epstein was then able to either make money on the various money markets with the knowledge he'd acquired. **Epstein's OVERT Business Model**.

But far more likely, was that he was engaged in a high level of international espionage and on-sold those secrets to international organisations or a range of international countries – **Epstein's COVERT Business Model**.

Now other than the money question, the other major question is how did Epstein attract all these rich, powerful and influential people?

I suggest that he used what I'm calling **"The Internet Guru Model"** long before the Internet Gurus even began appearing.

The Internet Guru Model

How many CEO's of significant bricks and mortar organisations do you feel as if you know personally? Probably NONE! Unless they're a personal or family friend, or a family member.

But with what I call **The Internet Guru Model**, a seemingly ordinary everyday person begins teaching a skill of some kind, selling a unique product, and offering an irresistible Free Opt-In Gift.

Then, thanks to the global reach of the Internet today, the sale of their classes or product, quickly starts bringing him or her in 8 or even 9+ figures a year.

The key to making that sort of money is that the "Guru" is the headline act. They teach and promote the skill, or sell their particular product, by **personally** appearing on camera to their followers on the Internet via video and/or **regular Social Media posts**.

The Result?

You get to know them really well, and very quickly, you consider the number one person in the organisation your personal friend. And if they take Q & As on their Zoom calls, they might even talk and interact with you personally, calling you by name, asking your opinion.

WOW how about that—they know me and even know my name.

And psychology 101 will tell you that there's no better way to make friends, or attract and keep a client, than that.

And that's what I suggest helped to make Epstein so popular, COMBINED, of course, with his irresistible "FREE Opt-In Gift".

Your "Free" Opt-in Gift

Yes, Epstein was even offering a "free opt-in gift". Hey mine is a free downloadable E-book.

But Epstein's opt-in gift was **free sex with an underage girl** or **a beautiful young woman.**

They'd be receiving those free "services" that Epstein himself had cultivated via **coercive control** and **sexual coercion.** And so the girls were **tried and tested first, and so guaranteed, by the Guru himself.**

Yes, all the girls and young women were guaranteed to satisfy the **post-pubescent debauched, sexual teenage-type fantasies** of these money-rich and powerful men, **at the psychological expense of the under-aged girls and young women.**

So "download" your FREE gift [sorry girl] now. When you do, you and I [Jeffrey Epstein in person] will become besties. You'll hang out with me, and meet my other rich and powerful playmates. We'll all hang out together at my incredibly fantastic parties, and I'll fly you on my very own plane, to my very own island.

All free of charge.

And once you're my bestie, **I'll play you like you've never been played before — subtly COERCING you into telling me your nation's secrets,** or organisation's **latest insider trading** information—**the COVERT aspect** of Epstein's Business Model in action.

You won't even know what's going on, until long after it's over.

It's all just the art of the deal, I believe it's called?

Now one **MALE researcher,** obviously a heterosexual male, was speaking on a video the other day. He'd just spent several days going through many of the Epstein Files. The other person, on camera, that he was speaking with, asked him about one very high profile name that appeared a number of times in the Files. And the researcher replied, oh he wouldn't be involved in any of the sexual activities because he's gay.

REALLY???

How naïve can anyone be? I'm sure Epstein was able to satisfy the predilections of **ALL of his "clients"** in that regard as well.

All of whom are victims.

But hey, who cares about the victims!

The victims remain the least protected stakeholders in this entire saga.

And by mid-February 2026, social media named at least two of Epstein's playmates who were, indeed, gay. *Surprise! Surprise!*

So while the spotlight of the Epstein Files is on the young girls and women that Epstein procured, I guarantee that many of these debauched rich and powerful men also craved the same "services" from young boys. Young boys who, as adult men, are a lot less likely than the women to come forward and say **yes "Me Too"**.

But in the last few weeks, that's exactly what has happened. Social Media is filled with talk of a man named, **Sascha Riley** (Sascha Borros), who gave an incredible 4-hour interview with journalist Lisa Noel Volding, in July 2025. It's true that his allegations have never been officially authenticated, but neither have a lot of the victim reports in the official Epstein Files. But most people who've listened to Sascha's interview say it is believable.

Sascha, a decorated Iraq war veteran, alleges that as a child he too was road-tested first by Epstein and one of Epstein's best friends before being trafficked to Epstein's playmates. He also opens a window into many alleged horrific crimes, and names names.

The interview, which has now gone viral on Social Media, was submitted to the police, and Sascha has agreed to testify in court. But to date, there's been no follow-up by authorities.

Why Not????

You'll find the URL containing the full 4-hour interview in this Endnote[22].

Personally, after listening to a couple of very short random grabs from different sections of the tapes, I chose not to listen to any more. It was far too upsetting.

All of those girls and women, as with any young boys, were just human commodities to be played with for the sexual gratification of these depraved rich and "powerful" men. The victims, whomever they were, were reduced to disposable instruments of gratification—warm blooded blow-up dolls.

Although a lot younger than Epstein when we were together, as I mentioned above, former husband **Josh was similarly sexually obsessed**. And so in retrospect, I recognise **those same warped patterns of behaviour** all too well. And my stomach churns.

Is it any wonder I became an ethicist???

And yes, while we're primarily hearing about Epstein trafficking girls under the age of legal consent—'cause those men *"like 'em young!"* **But frighteningly, please remember** that Epstein was no lone-wolf.

That same **manipulative, deviant coercion** has been, and no doubt still is, being perpetrated today, by many other perverted sexual opportunists, just like Epstein, who are **recruiting, coercing, and trafficking** thousands more victims, worldwide, only they're keeping a much lower profile.

As a dear colleague said: "When a system rewards predation and shields power, as seems to be currently happening, individuals become expressions of structural corruption."

Epstein's ***OVERT*** Business Model in Summary

Now that you have some ideas of Epstein's OVERT Business Model from a narrative perspective. Let me show you diagrammatically what it might look like.

And again, **this is purely a speculative model**, based on the vast array of dots appearing in the Epstein Files available to us all. I'll explain each "dot" in the table on the next page.

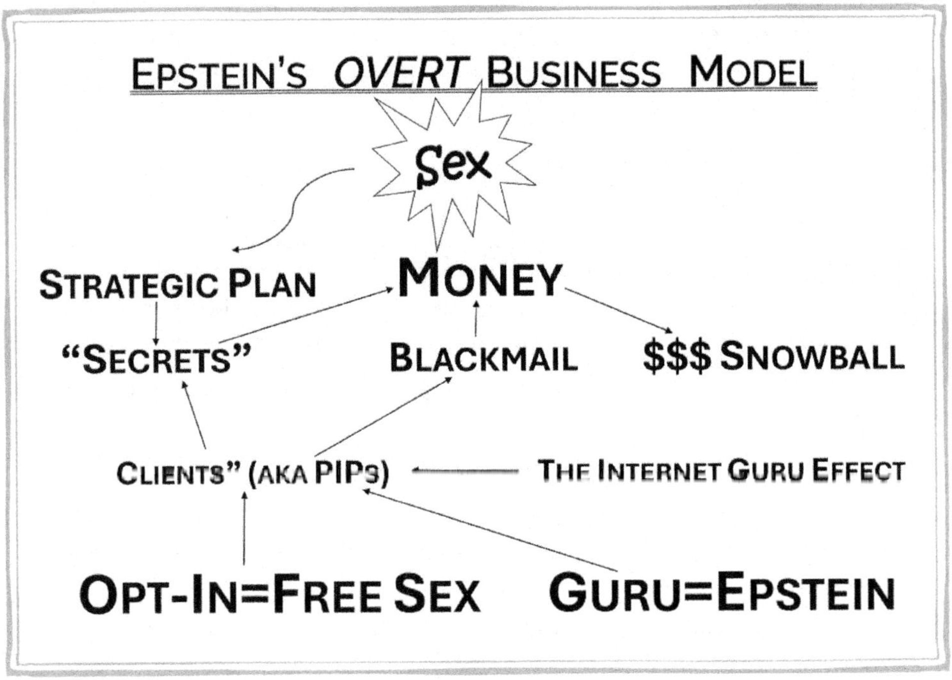

KEY TO EPSTEIN'S *OVERT* BUSINESS MODEL **Speculation** ONLY based on joining the Dots publicly reported and/or contained in the DoJ documents released so far – mid February 2026	
SEX	Starts with Epstein's Addiction to Sex, Money, & Power
STRATEGIC PLAN	... Meets Ghislaine Maxwell. Her father was a British media tycoon & alleged spy. Potentially double agent, or even triple agent allegedly working simultaneously for UK's MI6, the Russian KGB, and Israel's Mossad. He died "mysteriously" in 1991, aged 68. Officially, death was accidental, but potentially murder or suicide. • Potentially, this family culture could've led to the start of Epstein's alleged COVERT Business Model
CLIENTS=PIP [POWERFUL INFLUENTIAL PEOPLE]	Develop relationships with the most powerful, influential, and richest people worldwide—politicians, royalty, celebrities, corporate elites, etc via close 1-on-1 contact or "implied contacts" (*see below).
"SELL SECRETS"	• By developing a close personal relationship with PIPs, the charismatic Epstein could coercively elicit whatever trade, government, corporate, or any other secrets the PIP might have. • The alleged narcissistic, ego-filled PIPs would divulge these secrets to Epstein to allegedly impress Epstein to enhance their friendship even more. • Selling secrets such as those were probably Epstein's greatest source of income—other than ... • **If Epstein's COVERT Business Model** was in play, then virtually all secrets would be collected to go to that secret cabal.
BLACKMAIL	Around 2000 videos and 180,000 images were released by the DOJ on January 30th, 2026, with more to come. And with a major video surveillance system rigged up throughout his houses and the island, it's alleged that many or even most of the illicit sexual encounters were recorded. • Those who didn't have international espionage or trade "secrets" to divulge to Epstein to ensure their continued "friendship" could well have been blackmailed due to the videos Epstein had of them—**high level coercion 101**. • Once in Epstein's **coercive "web"**, the charismatic Epstein could potentially continue to **coerce** PIPs into divulging or hiding more of their secrets.

MONEY ??? **WEALTH ACCUMULATION**	**So where did all Epstein's billions come from???** • Directly from selling whatever secrets he could elicit from his PIPs, to the highest bidder. • Potentially from threatened blackmail • Snowball Investments— Gold, Bitcoin, Oil, etc—**Money Makes Money** • **OR if the COVERT** Business Model was a reality, then Epstein was just a very highly paid employee, with all his billion dollar + expenses fully paid for in return for his international espionage activities.
THE INTERNET GURU EFFECT	• The Internet Guru Model is described in the body of this chapter, above. • Just as money makes money, the richer and more powerful someone is, the more other rich and powerful people want to be included in their group. So this too has a snowball effect
• **IMPLIED CONTACT** is evident with Epstein writing emails to specific rich and powerful elites, but only sending the emails to himself. Or noting on his calendar appointments with PIPs, that never took place, or that were refused. This way the person is named in his documents, even though there was never any contact. This is yet another potential blackmail strategy.	

Moral Reflection on Coercion

If you are a victim/survivor of coercion linked to Epstein, or any similar network, and disturbingly there are plenty of similar networks throughout the world: The mere public exposure of these networks might not yet feel like justice to you. Justice requires accountability, and accountability requires **courage from institutions as well as individuals.**

So just as I suggested that Epstein might have had two business models running in parallel—his OVERT model and his COVERT model—so too something similar could well be happening with the release of the Epstein Files.

On one level, **international institutions** are beginning to investigate their elites—diplomats, royalty, business executives, and celebrities—for potential forms of alleged **international espionage**, and the alleged selling of **insider trading information**, and the like.

Ironically on another level, when it comes to Epstein's network, many of those same rich and powerful men who might have abused you, might also have been **victims of Epstein's coercion**—subjected to leverage, intimidation, and/or strategic compromise in one way or another.

And even though most of them have yet to be held to account for their actions, those perpetrators could well be having sleepless nights saying to themselves the very same words that you might have said yourself, to yourself: ...

- How could I have been so silly?
- How could I have fallen for Epstein's coercive and intimidatory tactics?
- How could I have put myself in this position?

Now I know that recognising any mental distress a perpetrator might be experiencing won't diminish or compensate for the trauma or suffering you experienced. And it certainly doesn't remove the legal, let alone moral, culpability of their actions.

However, it does highlight how **coercive exploitation** in any system such as **the legal system, political system, cultural system, and societal system** doesn't only harm the powerless. It moves upward as well as downward, infecting everyone it touches.

So the lesson of the Epstein Files is not merely about one man, or even about a circle of rich and powerful elites. It's about how easily systems can slowly decay and become corrupt if influence and power is permitted to override ethics and moral values.

And that notion is not new. The 1997 film, ***Wag the Dog,*** satirised a scenario in which a manufactured crisis—a war no less—diverted public attention from political scandal. And the Epstein Files are sure causing one heck of a political scandal at this time.

The movie highlights the idea that powerful institutional systems sometimes survive not by **resolving wrongdoing**, but by **redirecting attention** away from the problem at hand. The proposition being that a **major diversion is required — something emotionally larger than the scandal itself.** And as I'm sure you'd agree, nothing grabs public attention faster than a war, especially if your country is a major player.

So don't just sit and watch "The War" on TV as if it's the latest "reality" TV show — which of course it definitely is.

Instead, we must all remain vigilant and start asking questions about what's ***REALLY*** going on, and why, and with what intended outcome both for the war and also the diversion. Dismiss the social media propaganda. What's ***REALLY*** going on?

And so the question in this Epstein Saga, and all the other less prominent, yet equally perverted networks, is not only who will be prosecuted and when? It's what's required to change our overarching unethical societal systems, cultures, and perversions?

How can we **prevent coercion entrenched corruption** from embedding itself in society in the future?

This is not about revenge. It's about reform.

Coercion doesn't disappear when a single figure falls. It begins to dissolve only when **transparency, accountability, and moral courage** become structurally **NON-NEGOTIABLE** — **when institutions as well as individuals have the courage to shine a light on unethical actions.**

~ Chapter 7 ~
What Would You Have Done... REALLY?

Although I wish I'd have recognised the abuse earlier, talking to someone openly and honestly about what I have experienced helps me understand that I am not to blame.

~ DA Survivor – Anon ~

In Chapter 1, I said that I was writing this book, for the same reason as I wrote ***Brainwashed***. To defend victims, from the appallingly ignorant and totally unethical practice of insensitive victim-blaming. And so this chapter is probably the summit of this book. Not due to any great literary merit, but due to the ultimate intended message of the book, before moving on to the much more positive topics related to transformation healing and rebirth.

So let me begin with a little piece that I often include in my Conscious Change books if I'm about to say something that might be considered controversial. I call it my "Transparency Time" section. It prevents people from making false assumptions about me in relation to what I'm about to say.

Transparency Time

Overall, my entire life has been like an extended roller-coaster ride with extreme wonderful highs and the lowest of desperate lows, and then around it would go again.

I grew up in a privileged home with money. I went to a private girls only school and I mixed with the rich and the very rich. But even at the age of about 10 or 11, I was able to see clearly the difference between the girls, and also their parents, who handled their wealth with very impressive dignity—the state or quality of being worthy of honour or respect. Versus those who continually displayed "righteous entitlement"—an egocentric attitude someone has, believing they're superior to others and so automatically deserving of special treatment. They're often identified by their display of ostentatious wealth versus a much more dignified display of wealth.

So ostentatious wealth never impresses me. Indeed quite the reverse as evidenced in ***Brainwashed*** when I spoke about a couple of young men I was seeing when I was around the age of 19.

One man was the cousin of a school friend who drove around in a beautiful shiny red Alfa Romeo and co-owned his own business. The other drove a beat up old faded bomb that had to always be parked on the top of a hill so he could start the car each time by rolling down the hill. Apparently, it was more than just battery related.

Both men were good looking. And both men were former private school boys. So both originally came from homes with money.

However, on our first date, the bloke with the old bomb stopped off on the way home, leaving the engine of the car running of course. He dived into a shop and bought me a box of chocolates because he though I was such a lovely person and he'd loved the time he'd spent with me.

Now it wasn't even the chocolates that impressed me—although they were good. It was **the thought behind the chocolates** that meant so much to me.

I ended up saying good-bye to the flashy ostentatious Alfa driver and had a long term relationship with the other fella, even though we always had to find a hill to park on with each outing.

Having said that, over the years I've also dated some of the highest profile rich and most powerful elites. So I have a very good understanding of how the rich and powerful think, and act, and what's important to them.

It was always fascinating how often, not always, but on more than one occasion, the rich and powerful, both male and female, loved treating me like the love of their life, their very best friend, when things were going well for me and so I had something to offer. And yet refused to even talk to me when I ended up, for whatever reason, at one of those low points in my life.

But hey, I was the very same person.

Yet the people whose attitude to me **never changed**, were the poorest of the poor that I knew from Puppy Park. We all shared a common value, the great love of our dog/s, regardless of our wealth, or influence, or lack there of.

Similarly, when I was a university student, one of my part-time jobs was doing market research surveys over the phone. This was not phone selling, something I hate and don't condone, but market research with questions like who would you vote for if the Federal Election was held tomorrow, or which toilet paper do you prefer and why.

Now this was before the days of computers and so computer generated phone numbers. So at the start of each shift we'd go to the supervisor who'd hand out several sheets of phone numbers that we had to call that day. And without exception, **everyone hated getting the sheets of phone numbers from the expensive suburbs.**

Why?

Because, although not always the case, but the chances were so strong that we'd be treated badly, or even abused, by both men and women from the expensive suburbs. By contrast, the people from the poorer suburbs realised that everyone needed a job, and were always wonderful.

Again, not all the rich and powerful were like that. Many handled their wealthy situation with impressive dignity. BUT not all of them.

It makes for a fascinating study of the human condition.

Nevertheless, I've always said I'd prefer to be rich than poor. But not rich **at the expense of the poor**. And that's a big difference to keep in mind. Something all too many of the rich and powerful don't quite understand. Not even those who started out as one of the poor.

Needless to say one of my favourite sayings is in relation to humility: "Today's peacock might well be tomorrow's feather duster," as the former Prince Andrew can now attest to.

And the reason I share those stories is because near the close of the last chapter on The Epstein Files, in the section on "Moral Reflection on Coercion", I said that "Justice requires accountability, and accountability requires **courage from institutions as well as individuals....** Coercion doesn't disappear when a single figure falls. It dissolves only when **transparency, accountability, and moral courage** become structurally **NON-NEGOTIABLE"** in **institutions.**

Well it's now time to take a moral look at **individuals**. Not the victims, but the victim-blamers, who more often than not, are members of the rich and powerful elite.

Yes, there are some people, **interestingly normally women**, although again not always, who blame the victim for all the victim might have endured. They'll criticise the actions of these young women and under-aged girls and not their male perpetrators.

Here's a brief example of such a conversation on victim-blaming, that I had with a highly intelligent, professional woman who said it's the victims who are often to blame. And she gave the following example.

At the gym a few years ago I saw a pretty young woman on a treadmill, laughing and seemingly enjoying the company of the man who was standing in front of her.

He left shortly before me. And as I passed by the young woman, I said to her: "You looked like you were enjoying yourself."

She replied: "No way. He was a pig."

The woman I was talking with concluded the victim-blaming discussion by saying:

"Now it didn't lead to rape (as far as I know) but she was certainly leading him on."

To which I responded in amazement:

WHAT was she meant to do???? Say go away you pig??? Or even "no sir I don't wish to talk with you"????????? And yet she'd still have to see him every time she went to the gym?

Can't she just be her normal happy, laughing self, without it being seen as "leading a man on?"

But one of the worst examples of victim-blaming presented itself while I was researching the previous chapter. I watched a YouTube video of the program **Piers Morgan Uncensored**[23].

And believe it or not, but one guest on that particular episode left me more upset and angry than the horrific stories that were coming out of the Epstein Files themselves. Something that I'd have never thought was possible.

That guest was "**LADY**" Victoria Hervey, whose occupation in 2026 at the age of 49, according to Wikipedia, was "socialite".

WOW Socialite! Now that's a humanitarian type of "occupation" to be proud of, isn't it!

She doesn't appear to have ever married although she's known for dating many rich and powerful high profile men, including the former Prince Andrew. And she's also known for defending the rich and powerful men involved in the Epstein Saga, including the former Prince Andrew.

Now I'm very tolerant of those who have opposing views to mine. That's their right. And I'm certainly not the fount of all wisdom, unlike "Lady" Victoria, who continued claiming to be right about everything, and as a result she must also be right about the nothing-to-see-here-version of the Epstein Files too.

But I was even prepared to set all that aside.

Just as I'm **ALMOST** prepared to set aside two appalling comments she made as reported on Wikipedia[24]. The first does go back to 2003, when she notably said: "It's so bad being homeless in winter. They should go somewhere warm like the Caribbean where they can eat fresh fish all day." Maybe it was just a tongue-in-cheek comment in extremely poor taste. Without any context, I can't really say.

But another comment, on social media, for which there can be no excuses was after the death of Virginia Giuffre. She outrageously said of Virginia's death: "When lies catch up with you there's no way out."

Now I didn't think those comments could be topped, but they were in the Piers Morgan video. Talk about "pressing my buttons"!!!

Why?

Because with those comments and her following attitude, she epitomises the **"righteous entitlement"** that I find so absolutely deplorable, especially amongst the rich and powerful involved in this Epstein Saga.

A **righteous entitlement** that has left the rich and powerful believing that they can do what they like and will always be untouchable.

A righteous entitlement of privilege mistaken for virtue.

And so I keep putting inverted commas around the word "Lady" in Victoria Hervey's case because I'm sure that many would consider her words and attitude are a far cry from being a "lady", no matter who her father was from whom her title was inherited.

Now it's important to remember that reports from the Files indicate that Epstein specifically **targeted vulnerable young girls and young women**, particularly those from unstable or disadvantaged backgrounds. Why? **They were the easiest to manipulate and coerce.**

With that in mind...

"Lady" Victoria's attitude that really pushed me over the edge came in her defence of the rich and powerful, like the former Prince Andrew, who she claimed should be believed, versus the victims who were obviously liars. She said: "Can we talk about the quality of these girls?... The calibre of person we're talking about... ".

Her microphone was immediately cut off before she could be heard saying anything else.

It seems that her evidence for claiming the victims were liars was their disadvantaged backgrounds and social class compared to the social class of the rich and powerful men they were allegedly "accusing". After all, the rich and powerful men had said they'd "done nothing wrong", so obviously the victims must be lying. Simple as that!

Yet this latest tranche of documents includes photographs of the former Prince Andrew[25], kneeling on the floor on all fours (hands and knees) over the body of a young woman. An image many viewers have understandably found deeply disturbing and suggestive of predatory behaviour.

And **THAT'S the high social calibre** of human that "Lady" Victoria claims is the classy one to always be believed, as opposed to the young victim on the floor???

It does beg the question: How is "high calibre" Andrew doing these days?? In the shocking words of "Lady" Victoria herself, after the death of Virginia Giuffre: "When lies catch up with you there's no way out." I have to wonder if "Lady" Victoria should also take heed of her own words.

But sadly, "Lady" Victoria is far from alone with those views of hers.

In 2017 many women came forward with allegations of the sexual misconduct of a former chief justice of the Alabama Supreme Court and the Republican nominee in the U.S. Senate special election, Roy Moore[26]. He too had many victim-blaming supporters, including one high profile conservative evangelist who was interviewed on TV saying: "Between Roy Moore and the accusers, who is the more credible?"

Believe you me, it's the so-called accusers who are more credible!!!

Shortly after, the then US President Donald. J. Trump, said in Roy Moore's defence that the accusations were all "a big con job."[27] So again, Mr Moore was telling the truth and **the many women speaking out were all lying???**

And it's those views that are all, indeed, currently protecting the perpetrators. The rich and powerful protecting the rich and powerful.

As Virginia Giuffre courageously said[28] during a BBC interview, when asked about the former Prince Andrew, "He knows what happened.... I know what happened. And there's only one of us telling the truth."

I too can cite a great many first hand cases, where the richer and/or more powerful **<u>the men</u>**, the more likely they were to play fast and loose with the truth—"But I did nothing wrong" they'll continually protest.

My first hand experience is not only from personal lived experience, but also during my years as a sessional mediator/conciliator for the Departments of Justice.

The United States House of Representatives Committee on Oversight and Government Reform is currently running hearings into the Epstein Saga. Those called to testify, do so under oath, and so run the risk of prosecution for perjury if they lie. But has that ever really stopped anyone from repeatedly claiming "I did nothing wrong", no matter who they are?

Again, "Righteous Entitlement" with privilege mistaken for virtue.

But just remember, cover-ups rarely work.

So let's have a look at some of the things that these young girls and young women allegedly experienced, as reported in the files, and in interviews, that put them in such a traumatised state. Because if you're a victim-blamer, then I'd like to ask: **What Would You Have Done... *REALLY?***

A Scenario for those who Choose to Blame the Victims

If you're a victim-blamer, man or woman, I ask that you attempt to do something that might be very difficult for you to do.

Now assuming that you're not a black belt in Karate, I ask that you give some **serious thought to what you would have done in the same situation as these victims**. Especially 20 or 30 years ago, in a different world than we now have today.

So please imagine that **I'm now talking ABOUT YOU and what's happening TO YOU**. Not just relating a story **to you**.

I'm about to spend a few pages writing up **YOUR first-person narrative.**

So for the next few pages, this is YOUR life.

But first just a bit of **YOUR** background in this scenario.

You've come from an abusive home life of some kind. And whether that abuse was physical, sexual, or psychological like me, you are carrying around a great deal of **emotional, Childhood Conditioning baggage**.

At some level of consciousness, for some reason, **you consider yourself a "Total No-Hoper", "Damaged Goods"**. And this "Damage Goods" line, or something similar, is continually repeating in your brain.

But not to be beaten by your past, not only do you have the **courage**, but also **the burning desire** to really make something of yourself. You want to become a model, or an actress, or in Virginia Giuffre's case, a therapeutic massage practitioner.

Again, like me being enthusiastic to meet the high-profile UK entertainer when my TV producer took me to dinner: So too when a cultured woman takes the time to get to know you, you're over the moon **(Grooming 101).**

After all, growing up as you did, at a non-conscious level you believe you're just lowly "damaged goods" "a no-hoper" – that's what you've always been told. Yet here is this amazing woman, who, out of the blue, is actually interest in **YOU, and YOUR hopes and dreams**.

Or it could even be a school or college friend who asks you if you'd like to meet a man in the industry of your dreams. A man who can make your modelling or acting ambition a reality.

WOW, what an opportunity!!!

It's your opportunity to break-free from your current menial life. Finally, it's your big break. Of course you enthusiastically say yes. Who wouldn't say yes?

And so far so good.

So now to your first-person narrative. Although occasionally I will step in and make a comment or ask you a question.

Please, Take Deep Breath and Relax and actually re-live this first person story background of yours.

[YOU ~ YOUR 1st Person Story]

I'm driven to the home of this very special man by the cultured woman, who then takes me up stairs. I'm now in a closed or perhaps even locked room with a man who soon becomes naked. But the woman is still there.

Confusion sets in.

Surely it can't be as bad as it seems, especially as this nice woman is still here with me.

But now the woman begins **coercing me,** first to massage this man's naked body. She even shows me what to do—how to do it—what he likes.

She coerces me into removing my clothes and having sex with this man.

I don't want to do that. But what DO I do?? ***What CAN I do???***

[Stevie's Comment]

This situation is like someone who runs into a burning house to save the occupants. They're being called a hero. But would you have done that? You might like **to think that you would have. BUT you'll never know for sure until, or unless you're actually in that same situation, wearing those exact same shoes.**

The same applies here.

So please, continue to just sit quietly for a moment longer. Take some more deep breaths. And continue to imagine this very frightening situation ***YOU ARE IN.***

Think **HONESTLY: again *what CAN YOU REALLY do in this situation?*** Especially considering that you might only be a very young teenager. Or still a very young woman. Or for that matter even a much older woman. Your age is irrelevant. ***What CAN you REALLY do?***

[YOU ~ YOUR 1st Person Story]

Should I scream? But no one would hear me up here. And even if they did, no one will help me. This naked man is their boss. He pays their wages.

My thoughts are so jumbled and confused. My brain feels as if it's being scrambled — as if someone is attacking it with an egg beater.

Maybe, I could fight and struggle and kick him where it hurts the most.

But then I learned as a child that physically fighting in that way only leaves me being hurt even more. And there are two of them in the room with me. One or both would no doubt retaliate, if I try to fight.

[Stevie's Comment]

A number of victim-blamers say that you should just run out of the room at this point.

[YOU ~ YOUR 1st Person Story]

So *should* I try and escape and just run out of the room? I don't think that the door is locked. But aren't these two people going to restrain me? Or threaten me, again, in some even more frightening ways? And even if I make it out of the room, where am I going to run to?

The recruiter drove me here, so where would I go if I do escape?

[Stevie's Comment]

Please, just put yourself in that same situation.

This is traumatic stuff.

[YOU ~ YOUR 1st Person Story]

Come on girl, get your act together.

I wonder what henchmen Mr Epstein has lurking around the place who might physically hurt me if I do escape? And where could I hide?

And even if I get away, will the henchmen find out where I live and come after me or my loved-ones?

[Stevie's Comment]

Afterall, what specifically were **the coercive threats** made against you that made you comply with this naked man's wishes?

Just remember, one girl was threatened that her house would be burned down if she went to the authorities about what had happened to her. Another threat was: do what we say, or you'll continue to be raped.

Remember, these are the types of people you're dealing with.

This is no movie. This is REAL LIFE!!! And in this scenario **it's YOUR REAL LIFE.**

Like me, and my first #MeToo experience, sometimes compliance is the safest thing to do.

[YOU ~ YOUR 1st Person Story]

I've been locked in this room now for what seems like several hours.

And okay, now that I've completed my "task" they've given me some money for my "services".

So now, **I really AM "damaged goods"** So now what?

Well, this money sure beats what I was being paid as a cleaner, [or waitress, or whatever it was.]

So maybe I should just agree to repeat my "performance". After all, I've got no one to turn to for support or real help of any kind. No family to run to.

What am I REALLY going to do now?

[Stevie's Comment]

What WOULD you have done – REALLY?

And even though you survived that encounter, that doesn't mean that you don't hate yourself for doing it. That doesn't mean that you've not been **psychologically scarred for LIFE**.

And **who can you now trust? You can't even trust your own judgement any more?** After all **you trusted the cultured woman** and went in her car with her. So now what???

Suddenly, **at some level of consciousness**, everything spirals out of that **lack of self-trust**:

- ❖ A loss of real confidence
- ❖ A loss of complete safety
- ❖ A loss of focused clarity

- A loss of true direction
- A loss of meaningful purpose
- A loss of your powerful voice
- Most definitely a loss of your exciting dreams
- And yes, a total loss of your true identity

What WOULD you have done – REALLY?

I've looked into the stories of a great many victim/survivors, not only of Epstein, but victim/survivors of many other despicable men out there. **And there ARE plenty of them out there.**

And once again, those victim/survivors all talk about **a similar pattern of behaviour**. They were approached by a recruiter who found out what their dreams of the future were. On finding this out, the recruiter built great exciting images of how that dream could happen because the recruiter knew of someone in the industry who would help them **(again, Grooming 101)**.

Now, the scenario above, that I've just described might not apply exactly to all 1000 plus girls and women who fell into Epstein's trap, and the trap set by the **many other sexually debauched, high profile, narcissistic, money-rich, men who run similar schemes.** But the common patterns are always very similar.

That's why, for **your own sake**, it's so important not to negatively judge these young women until you know what you're talking about. Because if you do, **the only person who'll look foolish, ignorant, and definitely lacking in compassion, is you.**

Another incident to emerge from the current tranche of Epstein Files is something I alluded to above. The Epstein camp stole photos and negatives that one young girl had taken of her young 12 year old sister. The photos were distributed to Epstein's **sick and morally corrupt playmates**.

In **true coercive fashion**, the girl was threatened with having her house burned down if she reported the incident. Courageously, she did report it, **but the FBI took no notice**. Yet it is in the FBI's Epstein Files!

You'll recall from the previous chapter that many of the girls went to the FBI reporting some of the shocking things they'd been subjected to, not only by Epstein, but **by his money-rich, powerful, and depraved playmates.** But again, as we're now discovering, the FBI just filed the complaint away and took no further action.

WHY did that happen???

And by withholding two to three million further Epstein File documents, it seems as if it's still happening.

These are just some of the things currently being exposed with the drip-feed of Epstein Files.

Coercion by an unethical, evil perpetrator **is much easier than you might think**.

Justice begins the moment society refuses to look away: the moment society has the **moral courage** to start digging for the truth and openly expose the findings.

So before anyone is criticised for their actions, victim-blamers need to have the decency, even if they can't summon up the compassion, to think far more deeply than most people bother to do.

If you are a victim-blamer, do consider **ALL** the facts. **Put yourself in that exact situation**. And attempt to answer the question **honestly—what would you REALLY do <u>in that same situation</u>?**

You'll never know for sure unless you find yourself there, no matter who you are. As I often say: "I wouldn't wish **MY** life on my worst enemy."

So no one has any right to negatively judge any of these women.

Those who are still with us today are all true survivors.

And …

<u>Surviving takes Courage</u>.

~ Chapter 8 ~

Your Rebirth through Your Courage to Survive *AND* Thrive

I just want to tell other women that when you feel like you are falling there is a whole army of us ready to catch you. You don't need to explain because we have lived it, we know, we see, we are here for you ***and we believe you****.*

~ Shonagh CEO ~

If you've survived any form of abuse, **there IS a new life waiting for you**. A way to **turn your pain into purpose**.

By now, you might have realised that my book, ***Brainwashed,*** which was the genesis of this book, is **NOT just another self-help book. Not even just another memoir**.

And that's good, because if you're a victim/survivor of any kind of traumatic abuse, **that's not what you need**.

Most importantly, the three most important things victim/survivors need to know is that:...

1. They've finally found someone who understands them and what they've been through, that they can trust.
2. That they are believed.
3. And that they're not alone.

More than just my #MeToo experiences and the abduction and rape by the Catholic priest (above), if you're a victim/survivor, please know that I too might well have been where you have also been, in some form or another.

As I've said in one of my other books, my life has been akin to walking across a paddock and with each step I ended up in a cowpat (US aka—"cow pie").

For example, during my three-year marriage in my late twenties, I nearly lost my life on three separate occasions.

- Once, as I ran up my suburban street dodging gun fire—bang, bang, bang—from my husband's mistress. I was continually thanking ***Starsky and Hutch*** for teaching me to run in a zig-zagging fashion if ever bullets are heading my way.
- Another time after a very savage simultaneous, dual rape, I ended up in hospital with severe internal haemorrhaging and was told that as a result, I'd never be able to have children. Something I always wanted so very much.
- And as I've already mentioned in passing, a third occasion was when my husband at the time came up with his fast-money scheme. Easy! Take a half a million dollar insurance policy out on my life and then attempt to drown me in a rip in the surf.

  But as I'm here today you can tell that he was unsuccessful. The Universe sent a couple of men onto the deserted beach who braved the rip and saved my life. Although by the time they even entered the water, I was unconscious.
- Much later, as a radio broadcaster, a listener found it harder to just change the radio station, than to wait out side the studio for me to leave. As I walked out the front door, she jumped me, and with big knife in hand, attempted to kill me.

- ❖ And over the years, I've also been physically attacked and beaten on more than one occasion.

- ❖ Then, during a solo research trip to North Africa, I found myself repeatedly ordered—not asked, but commanded—to sit alone on the very last seat at the back of the bus. Until that moment, I had naively tucked the concept of segregated seating away into the pages of American history books, never imagining I would experience a modern-day echo of it myself.

  And it was during my two-weeks' stay in that country, that I was sexually abused on a couple of occasions. And far worse, I was sexually assaulted, physically, by a large group of 8-10 year-old boys. I had to literally, physically fight them off to finally escape. I also yelled a lot—very loudly—and came up with swear words that I didn't even know I knew.

  In retrospect, my act of physically fighting and verbally abusing young children was just as traumatic for me as was the actual ongoing sexual assault.

But where did those little boys learn to act that way?

- ❖ And as I mentioned in Chapter 1, I certainly know what it's like to be "victim-blamed" by ignorant people who heard my stories but for whom words like compassion, or understanding, or insight, were not remotely in their model of the world.

As a result, I can assure you, that I've repeatedly said to myself, the self-recriminating words that I've mentioned previously. Words that might be very familiar to you too, if you're a victim/survivor, or if someone you know, or love, is a victim/survivor.

Words such as:...

- "How could I have let this happen?"
- "Why didn't I see it sooner?"
- "Who am I NOW?"
- "How do I rebuild a life when I don't even trust my own choices?"
- "What if I really am broken in some way—***damaged goods?***"
- "What have I done wrong, AGAIN?"
- "What if I get it wrong, AGAIN?"

The problem that so many victim/survivors face is that they might have experienced years of psychological abuse, by one person after another. Or for others, they're still living with the aftermath of a single major abusive event—a trauma that will be with them non-consciously for life. Even so, they've courageously gone on **to become extremely successful in their life.**

But no matter how successful you've become since your life-changing experience/s. Or how well you've done in your working career: how lucky you've been with family and personal relationships: or how high your public profile has become. If you, like me, can relate to any of those self-blame thoughts above, perhaps you might also relate to the notion that once again, your main, core **wound is the collapse of your Self-Trust**.

At some level of consciousness, perhaps you don't trust your own judgement in certain areas of your life anymore. You might keep wondering who you really are and if you can fully rebuild the life you do indeed deserve. **Even if you no longer *think* you do deserve what we all deserve.**

So you don't just need a pat on the head and someone compassionately saying "you'll be OK". **It's not just about "healing".**

- You still need your genuine Self back.

- You still need your true power back.
- You still need your conscious future back.
- **And you still need your self-trust back.**

That's why I say that my book, ***Brainwashed,*** is not another self-help book, because ***Brainwashed*** doesn't do those self-help things, and neither does this book.

What ***Brainwashed*** does, is **expose the Anatomy of abuse—why you do/did what you did. Why you were able to be coerced as you might have been—as was I.**

In essence, ***Brainwashed*** explains your pain, gives you validation, clarity, and some words to focus on, for example:

- "Oh my God… it wasn't my fault."
- "This explains EVERYTHING."
- "I'm not crazy – I'm normal."
- "I'm not alone".
- "Someone finally **understands,** at a soul-deep level, because they've also been there."

In my later years, I **needed understanding** – for people **to really understand what I've been through.** That was probably what I needed the most in my life. And sure unless you too have been there, it's impossible to really understand. But at least to have the compassion to recognise that even though "I don't know for sure, but I can tell, that it must have been pretty terrible."

But where too from there?

Again, like me, you don't need self-help or just healing alone. Basically you need a soul-deep transformation—a rebirth and it's with that rebirth that comes the healing.

That's why I researched and wrote the Conscious Change Series of Books and put together their associated virtual Zoom programs, where you can learn the heart-centred life-skills that help you **rebuild your internal structure and your identity**.

They're designed to give you the possibility, the hope, and the skills to go out and make a difference in your world, as I've done in my world. So you can finally realise that: …

- There IS a way out.
- This is a journey and my ticket to my new life is right here.
- This is bigger than any trauma I might have experienced.
- YES!!! Like Lady Phoenix, I **can** develop **the courage** to rise from this.

YES!!!* If you've survived any form of abuse, there is a new life waiting for you, *if you want it.

As you're probably aware, **the ancient, majestic bird, the mythical orange phoenix,** is **the universal symbol of transformation, rebirth, and resilience.**

And so in my virtual Zoom workshop, **"Strategic Heart-Centred Leadership"**, and also my Book 7 ~ ***Conscious Feminine ENERGY*** and Book 8 - ***Conscious Leadership: Born of Heart-Centred Life-Skills and Global Wisdom***, you're introduced to **Lady Phoenix.**

Now, despite her angelic wings, she's not a religious figure, nor a mythic goddess. But just as Lady Justice, with her blindfold and scales is the iconic symbol of the legal system; Lady Phoenix is **the iconic symbol of transformation, in human form.** She's a symbolic metaphor for all of humanity, and especially victim/survivors, as she rises from the ashes of old paradigms and the past pain of abuse.

<u>MEET LADY PHOENIX</u>

And it's during the "**Strategic Heart-Centred Leadership**" workshop experience, that you begin to embody Lady Phoenix's **transformational *ENERGY***—heart-centred life-skills skills designed to help you reclaim your authentic identity and your quiet strength which is waiting within you.

What was once hidden begins to breathe again. What was silenced finds its voice. Your true identity reawakens as you rise from the ashes, not as someone new, but as the person you were born to be, empowered with courage, compassion, creativity, and curiosity—a radiant force for Conscious Change, touching lives simply by living from your heart-centre.

And as a **Heart-Centred Conscious Leader of Change,** you'll naturally lift and transform the lives of everyone you encounter.

Now you might say, but I'm not a leader. Or [worse still] I'm not a leader, look at the life I've led.

But oh yes, you really can be a leader in any area of your life that you choose—at home, at work, in the community, in society, or even the world at large.

Post Traumatic Growth

There's a relatively new field of study that I talk about in my Book 3 ~ *Conscious Self-Discovery*. It's called **Post-Traumatic Growth (PTG)**. And it's leading to an ever-increasing number of PTSD (Post Traumatic Stress Disorder) **sufferers** becoming **truly courageous PTSD leaders of change**.

With the right support and the right attitude, these new PTS survivors are discovering **tremendous positive growth** and a new motivating and meaningful life.

This new life is waiting for you not despite the life events you've endured, but BECAUSE of the life events you've endured.

So while *Brainwashed* is **the ANATOMY of abuse**; my Conscious Leadership work is the **ANTIDOTE for abuse**.

And this book *From Coercion to Courage* is the bridge you can cross to prepare you for **your transformation** as described in Book 8 ~ *Conscious Leadership* and in my **Strategic Heart-Centred Leadership** workshops.

It was certainly what I needed for **MY rebirth** too.

In essence, my Conscious Leadership work is about **soul-based ethical transformation, built on behavioural science and lived truth; inspired by the metaphoric *ENERGY* of Lady Phoenix** rising from the ashes of past pain.

It's created to help restore your identity, rebuild deep self-trust, and your inner compass, and design a future grounded in ethical leadership, purpose, and heart-centred power, so you can indeed become **a heart-centred conscious leader in any area of your life.**

With your new courageous identity, you'll become the conscious leader that the world is waiting for to go out and **transform the lives of all those that YOU connect with**.

Yes, you can move from ...

- "I survived"... to **"I create".**
- From: "I don't know who I am"... to **"I know exactly who I choose to become."**
- From: "I hope my life gets better"... to **"I'm designing an ethical/conscious future aligned with my purpose, and power.**
- From "I'm just a victim" ... to **"I AM a Conscious Leader of Change, making a real difference to the lives of all those I interact with".**

And sure—Success takes Courage

But it can also be very exciting

Meanwhile, if you want to find out more about **"conscious/ethical leadership"**, my Book 1 ~ ***Conscious Change for an Ethical Business, Life, and World:*** *An Introduction* *to Conscious We not Me Change and the Conscious Change Series in Review* is waiting for you as a free download, when you go to https://www.StevieCarnegie.com and just scroll down a bit.

Also, in **Appendix A, following,** you'll also discover some insight into the **transformational journey** that awaits you, if you so choose.

~ Chapter 9 ~

The Courage to Rise When No One Claps

Experience without theory is blind, but theory without experience is mere intellectual play.

~ Immanuel Kant ~

In this book, you've been briefly introduced to a number of my life-experience stories. And in this closing chapter, I'd like to start with something far less "exciting", but as with everything I do in life these days, I have an important reason for doing it.

So please stick with me here and by the end of this chapter it will have become clear why I wanted to share the following bit of my background.

Actually, the chapter quote above, from Immanuel Kant, will give you a clue as to where we're headed.

Keep in mind that I left school at the end of 9th grade, when I was just 15. And at that time, I'd had hardly even ever read a book—books were boring. Today, I have a much reduced library of over 6000 books, all of which I've read, or partially read. A few years ago, my personal library had grown to close to 12,000 books, but due to a lack of space, I reluctantly had to do a major culling job.

From leaving school in 9th grade, I didn't start as a 1st year undergraduate university student until I was almost 40 years of age.

The big picture is that I ended up as a **Moral Philosopher**. Then chunk down a level, and more specifically **I'm an Ethicist**, especially related to environmental ethics, business ethics, and of course leadership ethics with my main focus underpinning them all being **Virtue Ethics**. All of which is reflected in the title of my PhD thesis/dissertation, ***Heart-Centred Virtue Ethics: Raising Ecological Consciousness in Organisations***.

Now as is common practice, at the start of my PhD work all doctoral candidates had to attend a series of seminars telling us what to do, how to do it, and what to expect, as well as what was expected of us. And one such talk was to instruct us that ideally a PhD will focus on a very detailed, narrow aspect of the area in which we were going to work. So if you're interest in parrots, keep your doctoral work to a very specific aspect of a parrot: maybe the colour of the beak of a specific kind of parrot.

Now okay, if I need a critical eye operation, I only want to be worked on by a surgeon who has very detailed knowledge of the human eye. Not someone who just says, yeah well, the kidneys are there. And a little higher and you'll find the lungs. Above that, the head should be on top of the shoulders and in the head I'll find a couple of eyes, one of which I have to operate on. ***NO!!! NO!!! NO!!!***

So detailed specialists are essential in our world of wonder.

But at the time I began my PhD, my 40+ year life-experience had taught me that the world also needed people with a much broader understanding of our world.

With great determination, I **"courageously"** fought the system for what I believed was necessary **to stay true to my future** "save the world" plans.

It was almost impossible to get my proposal accepted by the academic powers-that-be, but after a great deal of negotiation and persistence, eventually I won.

My thesis/dissertation was a multi-disciplinary research PhD from fields as diverse a moral philosophy, applied ethics, environmental philosophy, social science, behavioural science, psychology, environmental education, ecofeminism, environmental management, and business management, with virtually all topics written from an ethical perspective.

And I'm glad to add that unlike the mid 1990s, these days a multi-disciplinary PhD project is quite common. Yes, that side of our world has significantly changed for the better too.

Now I did have to find an umbrella supervisor who'd sign off on all the on-going administration's paperwork. I also had to find a whole mob of different supervisors for each of those different fields, or thesis chapters, that I'd put together.

And truth be told, actually I did go through three of those umbrella supervisors over the course of my work, because they were each so unfamiliar with a lot of what I was attempting to do. Although I must say that ***I*** always thought it was all pretty straight-forward and basic common sense. Heck, I wasn't trying to find a cure for cancer.

But for all of that determination and persistence, it's still my **life-experience and not my PhD**, or the rest of the alphabet soup after my name, that has helped me **survive today, as I have**.

Nothing can beat good old life-experience. **BUT** you must combine that life experience with some solid analytical skills that you should be able to learn in a university or some form of tertiary college. Alternatively, you need to have the egoless **courage to turn to, and listen to,** someone who has those multi-perspective analytical skills if you want a wining combination.

Similarly however, the academic rigor without the **courage and openness** to learn from other life-experience skills will get you no further than the walls of academia.

Again as Immanuel Kant said in the chapter quote above: "Experience without theory is blind, but theory without experience is mere intellectual play".

When you have the **ego-less courage to understand** the importance of **both life-experience AND multi-perspective academic rigor**, then you really are ready to change the world.

Now throughout this book, and especially in this final chapter, I keep using the word **courage.** So why is that? **And what IS courage really all about?**

What is Courage?

There are those in this world who think that a word like "tariff" is the most beautiful word in the English language. For me, it's a close call between, **love, truth, peace, and courage.** And unlike "tariff", love, truth, peace, and courage are all **ethical virtues.**

Historically, courage has been primarily about **facing your fears**. And so it was always linked to men, and their military service. Men who go to war and **face the FEAR of dying** for their country. And even when an increasing number of women joined the different military "forces", for some reason the word courage was still more often aligned to men rather than those equally courageous women: but that's a story for another day.

Life itself can also be a battle that we need **the courage** to get through, and so for those of us who have **"the courage" to acknowledge that we now live in a changing world,** courage has taken on a totally different and much broader, but equally important role, as you'll soon discover.

Courage, which is sometimes referred to as **bravery**, or **intestinal fortitude**, or **guts**, or **as having other parts of the MALE anatomy**, is a **complex virtue**. And so before exploring the word courage more deeply, it's probably important to spend a moment explaining what a virtue is.

So First, What is Virtue?

The word "virtue" is a commonly used word generally referring to something good. And while that's an accurate description, there's a lot more to virtues than that. So stay with me.

In 1999, I was one of only three delegates from Australia to attend the first International Conference on Emotional Intelligence for practitioners, held in Chicago.

As I listened to speaker after speaker at the conference, I began to think ***these people aren't speaking about the social science of emotional intelligence, they're all speaking about Virtue Ethics.***

Interestingly though, **THEY** didn't realise they were talking about Virtue Ethics as was confirmed when I spoke to a number of the high-profile speakers during breaks.

It's a bit like the first **UN World Happiness report**[29], which says that "happiness research needs to **restore Virtue Ethics"**, when Virtue Ethics is [seemingly unknowingly] already embedded in most of the happiness research. It's just that social scientists don't always realise it, as I discovered at the Emotional Intelligence conference.

But before continuing, as a Virtue Ethicist, let me acknowledge any potential bias that you might (rightly) perceive whenever I talk about virtues, including courage. And after you've read this chapter you can decide for yourself if Virtue Ethics—**ethics from within**, is as important as I believe it is.

You can find out more, specifically, about Virtue Ethics in my Book 5 ~ ***Conscious Love:*** *Cultivating a Consciousness of Virtue-Based Love for a More Peaceful, Loving, and Sustainable World* and also an ethics overview in Book 2 ~ ***Conscious Intelligence Competencies,*** Competency #5—Ethics-in-Action.

The main form of ethics in the Western world is, what's known as, **Rules-Based Ethics**. So if you want to be an ethical person, you'll obey the customs and rules imposed by the society in which you live. So I call Rules-Based Ethics, **Ethics from Without** or imposed by the culture and society outside of you.

By contrast, **Virtues Ethics is Ethics from Within** and is **based on developing character traits** that'll help you fulfil your highest potential as a human interacting and living on a planet with billions of other humans.

Both Rules-Based Ethics and Virtue Ethics have an important role to play in our society. But just because someone follows the rules when people are watching, doesn't mean that they're necessarily an ethical person.

By contrast, to be considered an ethical person based on **Virtue**, they must have a **good character** and do good things because that's what their heart **wants them to do**, and not just what society **tells them to do**.

Interestingly, in very recent times, progressive schools are introducing students to a subject that generally runs over middle school, and the first few years of high school. The subject is generally called **"Character Education"**.

And just like today with the word **"Conscious"** being used instead of **Ethical**; so **Conscious Leadership**, Conscious Parenting, Conscious Business, when we're actually talking about **Ethical Leadership**, Ethical Parenting, and Ethical Business and so on, Character Education is the same sort of thing.

Character Education is actually all about **Virtue Ethics** by a different name.

Virtue Ethics is one of the oldest forms of ethics and was taught by the ancient Greeks over two and a half thousand years ago, as well as in the ancient Eastern philosophies.

And **Courage** is considered to be one of the four most important virtues one can possess. As such, it's known as a **Cardinal Virtue**, together with **Prudence**, **Justice**, and **Temperance.** So what are those three virtues all about? And I'll come back to courage in a minute.

I often refer to **Prudence** as "street smarts" or the everyday wisdom to know **what the best thing to do is** in any given situation—**keeping in mind the potential outcome** of your chosen actions.

Unlike prudence, in it's simplest form, **Justice** is not about knowing the BEST thing to do, but **the RIGHT thing to do** in any given situation—what is fair to all parties. And of course in theory justice forms the basis of our court system.

Then **Temperance** is about self-control in all things that you do, think, and feel. So moderation in all things. And that's why the word temperance is often linked to a moderation in the consumption of alcohol to prevent acting in inappropriate, anti-social ways.

Now there are two main umbrella forms of virtue. They are **Moral Virtues and Intellectual Virtues**. Moral Virtues are the way you act, what you do, Ethics-in-Action if you like. While Intellectual Virtues are to do with the way you think.

You'll find the following image in a number of my books showing you some of the most common **moral virtues**.

CONSCIOUS LOVING ACTIONS ~ ETHICAL VIRTUES

These moral virtues/conscious actions include, but are not limited to:

Empathy, Equality, Respect, Trust, Compassion, Truthfulness, Integrity, Fairness, Gratitude, Altruism, Kindness, Co-operation, Justice, Giving, Mercy, Peace, Joy, Acceptance, Non-judgement, Patience, Courtesy, Generosity, Benevolence, Courage, Temperance, Nurturing, Honesty, Humility, Selfless-Self-Love, Self-Control, Conscious Sustainability, &

***We not Me*—Conscious Living**

And just like it's essential to have, or have access to, **both life-experience AND rigorous, multi-perspective, analytic skills**, it's just as important to possess **both moral and intellectual virtues**, which could be argued are the same as life-experience (Moral Virtues) and analytical skills (Intellectual Virtues).

Keep in mind that **moral virtues** like compassion, kindness, and respect, might be what your heart wants to do. But it's the **intellectual virtues** like practical knowledge (also known as prudence or street smarts), wisdom, science, understanding, and intuition that will help you decide if those heart-centred actions are appropriate or not.

For instance, if you meet someone living in poverty, **your compassionate [Moral Virtue] heart** might want to help them by giving them some money. But is that really the right way to really help them?

This is where your **intellectual virtues need to step in**. What is the best way to help that person? Is it by just giving them some money? Well that'll depend on their actual situation. So is it better to give them a job so they can earn some money? Or teaching them a skill, so they can get a job?

With each of those ideas, you're still helping them in a **compassionate manner [moral virtue]**, but your **intellectual virtues** will help you decide the very best way to help them.

Back to Courage

Now unlike most virtues, courage is a **complex virtue from a dual perspective**.

First, courage can be both a **moral virtue**, so something heart-centred; and **also an intellectual virtue** meaning that it can guide your heart-centred desires.

For instance, from a **Moral perspective**, it's about having the courage to face danger; to do something that you'd prefer not to do; or to speak up about an important issue that you feel strongly about when you know there are those who might disagree. Such as me having the courage to continually speak up and fight the academic hierarchy to get them to agree with my multi-disciplinary PhD.

And from an **Intellectual perspective**, courage is about having the strength of character and wisdom to hold back from acting on your heart's desire, and first question whatever it is before acting.

Or using those multi-perspective analytical skills **[intellectual virtues]** that I spoke about, to decide if you should take whatever action your heart desires **[moral virtue]**, in the face of adversity and opposition. So **the courage** to follow your heart's desire, despite what others might think of you. Or the possibility that your heart's desire might even be wrong. This is certainly something that many politicians could do well to learn.

Then the **second reason** that courage is consider **a complex virtue** is that it's often referred to as an **enabler or facilitator virtue**. You see courage can work alongside any of the other virtues to ensure that you actually follow-through and demonstrate those other virtues in an appropriate fashion.

So the **courage to** **respect** [moral virtue] the role a person holds even if you don't respect their actions or character. **Alternatively,** the **courage to speak out** **honestly** [moral virtue] against someone's action, regardless of the role or position they hold. Both are ethical actions. Which one would you choose to follow?

This is why it's so important to have the **courage to** **wisely** [intellectual virtue] assess the situation from both your **lived-experience** **AND** **a multi-perspective analysis**.

You really can have some fun games playing with all of this!

The Expansion of Courage

Even today, courage is still mainly thought of from a physical perspective, such as the courage to run into a burning building to save a child if you're a fire fighter. The courage to pick up the pieces of a broken body in an attempt to save a life if you're a paramedic. Or the courage to say no, I will not commit an unjust or inhumane act, if you're a soldier or a marine in a war zone, even if ordered to do so. Remember, the Nuremberg, or "Superior Orders" Defence[30] is inadmissible on most occasions. So to disobey an order, **takes real courage, both moral AND intellectual courage.**

But as I mentioned near the start of this chapter, in this 21st century, courage has greatly expanded beyond the physical courage associated with your profession. It's now essential for both women and men to have **the moral courage to open yourself to vulnerability**, combined with the **intellectual courage** to know how much of your vulnerability to show and to whom.

Now as you might, or might not, be aware, my Book 7 ~ *Conscious Feminine ENERGY*, is about feminine ***ENERGY***, not feminism, but the **ENERGETIC traits** most commonly associated with women. But these days, these traits are becoming more common **in courageous men too**—which is wonderful. Exactly what the world needs at this time.

These **Female Energetic TRAITS** that I mention in other books include moral virtues like a ***we not me*** focus, partnerships, love consciousness, peacemaking, power-with not power-over, co-operation, tact, agreement, consultation, discussion, intuition, the abstract, patience, nurturing, creativity, diplomacy, and consideration, as well as music, imagination, wholistic right-brain thinking, and a wholistic spiritual view of the world.

And symbolically, feminine-energy is associated with the number two, the moon, water, circles, curves, and swirls. All of which are represented on the cover of Book 7 ~ ***Conscious Feminism ENERGY***.

- **So today, courage** now includes a totally different and much broader, but equally important role. Such as **the**

courage for men to also embrace those feminine **ENERGETIC TRAITS, not necessarily feminism, but those energetic traits,** the benefits of which are highlighted in Book 7 ~ *Conscious Feminine ENERGY*.

- **So today**, everyone must develop **the courage** to tell the truth. After all, without truth there are no facts. Without facts there can be no trust. And without trust, deep love and relationships do not exist.

- **So today**, we must all summon **the courage** to be open and vulnerable enough to tell someone you love them—never miss that opportunity. After all, no matter how old or how young they might be, their life could be extinguished at any time—we never know.

  Then **the courage** to accept what someone says to you without fear or without condemning them. But instead the **courage** to discuss how it is for you and the **courage** for you each to negotiate the best course of action from there.

- And it's important to have **the courage** to accept rejection and take it as a learning experience.

  When I was looking for my first main radio job, it was long before computers, the Internet, and email. And I sent out snail mail letters to radio stations all over Australia and ended up with a folder almost 2 inches think of rejection letters. The fact that I was a woman didn't help my cause at that time either. But with each rejection letter came a learning experience and so growth that prepared me for the next round of letters.

- It's also essential to have **the courage** to discuss a topic openly and honestly. Now sure, traditionally most women are better at that than are men. But it's one of the most important areas for peace and harmony at home, at work, and for the world.

And it all starts with ***COURAGE***.

But before giving you some examples of **courage, and lack of courage-in-action**, you'll recall that at the start of this chapter I said that "historically, courage has been primarily about facing your fears." But courage is more than **"primarily"** facing your fears, but it's almost **exclusively** about **facing your fears**. That's because fears are so pervasive.

As a result, everyone in our world of relationships, but especially victim/survivors of any form of traumatic event, need to have a basic understanding of fear, if they're to develop the **courage to survive and thrive, and move forward**.

Facing Your Fears

True courage is not the absence of fear, but the mastery of fear. Of acting despite feeling afraid—after your intellectual virtues have looked into the situation-whatever that situation might be.

And sure, we all know what fear is like as an emotion when we experience it. But **a little understanding of fear** can be a big help in mastering the idea of fear and overcoming past abuse and **living a courageous life in the future**.

Now we can have surface-level fears, when we're well aware that we're feeling afraid of something. However, we can also have deep-seated, non-conscious, fears that we're less aware of, but that can lead to inappropriate actions, which I'll talk about in a minute.

While all fears are based on an emotional reaction to something, when I talk here about fear, I'm not referring to a physically-triggered "oh there's a snake" type of fear. Or someone is shooting at me type of fear. Sure, in those cases be afraid, "be very afraid" and do what you have to do to survive.

But those sorts of physical fears are not very common for the average person.

And you know something very interesting that I can attest to from personal experience **on more than one occasion.** In **the moment** when we're faced with a genuinely deadly situation, like being shot at, for most people our survival mechanism kicks in, and we don't actually feel **the emotion of fear** at all at that time. It's more **the intellectual aspect** of **what on Earth do I have to do to survive this**.

Sure, **after** the life-threatening event you could experience some very negative emotions which can even result in Post-Traumatic Stress Disorder (PTSD).

However the emotion of fear is normally the product of an ***anticipated*** threat, which more often than not has no foundation.

Even Aristotle, all those years ago, taught us that, with his words: **"Fear is pain arising from the anticipation of evil."** And for most people, genuine fears are, thankfully, very rare, while the fear of an ***anticipated*** evil event is extremely common. And that's when we need to **summon up the courage** and **face that fear**.

That **anticipated fear** will more than likely be a social-type of fear that could well be linked to having experienced a past traumatic event, and you're experiencing a form of "flash-back". Or it could be a fear that's linked to a limiting belief which might or might not be a legitimate belief.

For instance, it could be a social fear associated with a fear of people who are different to you – who have different beliefs, or a different culture to you. Or even just an anticipated fear of interacting with others for whatever reason.

Indeed, these anticipated "social" types of fears can be superficially based and triggered by anything at all that's going on in your life.

So, dig, dig, dig, moving down one level at a time.

Fear → Limiting Belief/Anticipated Threat → Original Cause [this could be childhood conditioning, or past abuse, or even a form of abusive military training] **→ Courage to Face the Fear**

Activity 1: Cpt 9—Emotionally-based Fears

1. Make a list of all the times when YOU personally have been afraid.

2. And after each fear, write WHY you were afraid—what specifically you were afraid of. Or what specifically were you afraid might happen?

3. Now go through those fears and mark which ones were legitimate fears, and which ones were fears due to your ANTICIPATION that something untoward might happen to you.

Just one point to keep in mind. Trying to work out what the fear is all about while you're actually experiencing the emotion is not always the best idea. But it **is** essential to reflect back and get to that underpinning negative or limiting belief **after the event** is well and truly over. And then once you're at the limiting belief level, it will be easier to keep digging down, down, and get to that original conditioning **[the cause]** that led to the fear response **[the symptom]** and then address it as soon as you can.

Briefly, the limiting beliefs that trigger these fears will usually, although not always, but usually have something to do with you feeling your basic **human needs** are being threatened in some way. And you can find out more about your basic human needs in Bk 3 ~ *Conscious Self-Discovery*.

Meanwhile, this might be a fear of losing your job, or losing someone you love. Or the fear of losing your home. Or the fear of having someone discover a long-held secret you've been keeping. Or the fear of appearing weak in the eyes of others. Or the fear of losing control of a situation. Or worse still, the fear of losing control-*over* someone.

It might be that you want to demonstrate that you're in control in a work situation—so you're the boss and you expect your employees to obey you. Or in a domestic situation, you expect your children to do what you tell them to do and if they don't, you yell at them, or heaven forbid, you hit them until they do obey you.

So which specific needs of yours are under threat by these people, or this situation that has triggered your fear? And that's not a rhetorical question.

As with all limiting beliefs, it's essential to keep digging down to get to the truth of the matter.

So the number one key is to **ask questions** of yourself, and do some independent investigation and get to the genuine facts, so you **understand** [Intellectual Virtue] what's really going on, externally around you. Do you really need to fear someone because they have a different coloured skin to you, or they speak with a different accent?

And whatever you do, don't just rely on Facebook's fake news and false facts. Chat GPT can be a good start, but even then you'll still need to do some more **multi-source fact checking**.

It's essential that you get to the heart of the truth about "the situation", whatever that situation might be that **triggers your fear**. And **also** dig down and get to the truth ***about your feelings associated with those particular fears***.

If you're a victim/survivor of any traumatic event, then on the surface, the reason for your fear will probably be obvious. And that's a great start.

But you still need to dig, dig, dig to determine if your subsequent or current fear, is based on a correct or an incorrect belief or assumption associated with your very original fear. Or is this current superficial fear, as the word fear sometimes implies, just...

False
Evidence
Appearing
Real

Once again, remember that your **feelings of fear** are yet another **symptom** of an underlying **cause** that generally stems from some form of negative conditioning, or brainwashing, or coercion, or traumatic event—this could be due to childhood conditioning, or past abuse, or even a form of abusive military training. And if you dig even deeper, you'll probably discover that your greatest fear is losing a "human need". And I talk about human needs in Book 3 ~ ***Conscious Self-Discovery***.

And so like all unsupportive emotions and behaviours, it's important to do that digging, to work out what that cause is. Then you have to decide if there is a legitimate reason for your fear, or is it the long-term memory embedded in your brain that's just saying: "Hey you went through something terrible before, so just checking to see if it could possibly be happening again."

As an example, **PTSD is often known as the Disorder of Avoidance** due to the sufferer being "**trapped in a state of extreme fear,** or **guilt,** or **shame"**. So silencing someone will become an automatic habit if a PTS sufferer suddenly **fears** someone is about **to say something** that **they're afraid to hear**.

This fear could be linked to the fear of hearing something that will make them feel **guilty**, or **embarrassed**—two very common feelings that PTS sufferers will easily experience.

Or they might be **afraid** that the speaker might want to chastise them about something. So **silencing the speaker**, to **avoid hearing** what the speaker will say, will mean that they won't "get into trouble--AGAIN".

This can be a strong reason for avoiding hearing what the other person has to say if the PTS sufferer is the victim/survivor of childhood abuse.

And as a PTS sufferer myself, **I know exactly what those fears can feel like.**

They're absolutely terrible, they really are. Sometimes my insides feel as if they're about to be ripped open. And my stomach feels as if it's reached my throat.

For me, it's normally about **the fear** that I'm about to **"get into trouble"** for something. AND SO, I **just do NOT want to go there**. And yes, as I spoke about in ***Brainwashed***, I did experience childhood/teenage psychological abuse, and continually got into trouble for things I'd not done wrong.

But I am so lucky that as part of my "rebirth" I've done the PTSD research that I have and so have the background understanding of PTSD that I have, together with all the personal development work I've done over the decades. That has all enabled me to push through those extreme fears when I'm about to **confront a situation I do NOT want to deal with—normally a face-to-face personal "discussion".**

Sure, to this very day I STILL experience all those initial very negative, stomach churning, anxious feelings, and fears that I'm about to "get into trouble" ***AGAIN***, if I'm having to confront a personal situation—those fears rarely go away. **And I hate it.** I'd much prefer to hide under a rock somewhere, where no one will be able to find me.

However, by **summoning up the courage** to push through, **despite those fears** and the very **strong avoidance mechanism kicking in**, the **most exciting thing** can normally happen.

First, and I'm very serious in what I'm about to say: first make sure that you know that the other person is not about to kill you or physically harm you in any way. That'll call for a totally different strategy.

But then, by summoning the courage to push through those fears, and listen to what someone needs to say to you, and then respond as calmly as possible and **discuss the matter**, you'll frequently come out the other side not only **feeling empowered,** but **with a totally new perspective on the matter.**

You could well have discovered a new truth that will completely **free you from any potential guilt regarding the matter whatsoever.**

The more you can **find the courage to avoid avoidance** and accept your situation and **work with it, instead of fighting it or hiding from it** all the time, the happier you'll be. And the more successful you'll be.

And yes, PTS sufferers can indeed be very happy and very successful if they choose to be. Afterall, as the old saying goes, "what doesn't kill you will make you stronger". And although that's a rather trite throw away line, it does have some merit.

Also, when a PTS sufferer silences someone, what they are actually doing is committing a form of **psychological abuse**. And surely after all they've been through, the last thing that they'd really want to be is an abuser themselves.

Negative or Anti-Social Actions based on Fear

As I've said many times, fear is at the foundation of virtually all negative emotions.

Give me **a negative emotion** or **an anti-social action** and some **time to dig**, and **I'll tell you what you're afraid of**. And from there, **if you have the courage**, we can work out if it's a legitimate fear to have, or not. And if it's a legitimate fear, what can be done to work around it, or overcome that fear.

I think that I must have been born to do that sort of work. Because I can clearly remember, as a 10 year old at school, when we were all lined up waiting to go into an exam room, I'd be surrounded with class mates. They'd all be saying **how afraid they were** at having to do the exam. And I'd work with each of them asking them the questions necessary to discover exactly **why they were afraid** of the forthcoming exam, and **how they could handle that fear**. I always thought it was great fun.

But if you're one of the millions of people who've experience some form of psychological or emotional abuse, unless the perpetrator has a diagnosable psychiatric condition, then chances are that if someone digs down deeply enough the perpetrator will discover that they treated you that way due to some **deep-seated fear they're living with and yet don't have the courage to address**.

Emotional Abuse —[DIG]→ Limiting Belief —[DIG] → Deep-Seated Fear —[DIG] → Original Cause [potentially Childhood Conditioning, or an abusive relationship] **—[DIG] → Courage or Not, to Face that Fear**

An obvious example of these deep-seated fears is my brother **coercing my mother [Emotional Abuse-Elder Abuse 101]** into handing over all the properties—one-by-one—that my father left her when he died. (See Chapter 2 above).

Was my brother a criminal or a "bad" man, or did he have a diagnosable psychiatric condition? The intellectual side of me says, "no".

So what was his **limiting belief** and **big deep-seated fear** that he didn't have **the courage to face?**

And this is a very simplistic answer to a very complex question. But here goes.

Basically, he was totally **obsessed with a need to have a successful business and make lots of money**. Sound familiar??? It's an obsession many people have.

Yet he didn't have the business skills, or knowledge to achieve that aim and was **too egocentric** to listen to those who might be able to teach him what to do.

So **his greatest fear** was that unlike his father (our Dad), **that he would fail in his greatest life-long desire—to have a successful business and make lots of money**.

As he continued to burn up money in his business in unethical and almost **addictively extravagant ways**, his answer was **to coerce my mother [unethical, anti-social Elder Abuse**

101] to keep replacing what he'd lost by selling up her properties and giving him the money from each sale.

His **limiting belief** being that all he needed was a bit more capital, and a bit more capital, and a bit more capital and the business would thrive. **A totally incorrect belief**. What he really needed was **the courage to say I have no idea what I'm doing, can someone please teach me.**

But then his little sister, **me**, got in the way by attempting to convince her mother to stop selling up all her properties and handing the money over to him. And **he was afraid** that I'd succeed and my mother would stop selling her properties.

So **he had to get rid of me**. The obvious way would have been to kill me. But at least that was beyond him.

Instead, he concocted this elaborate tale that as I was the company's bookkeeper, I was the cause of the company losing money by embezzling it all in one form or another.

First he had the job of convincing my mother of that story. And that was indeed easy as she adored him, and didn't think much of me—my arrival was a real accident that she certainly never wanted.

However, once my mother was on board with my brother's fictitious story about me, the rest, as they say is history. My mother then spread the word far and wide about her shameful delinquent daughter. And all family and friends said: "Well ... it must be true seeing as Stevie's own mother says it's true and is openly telling us all about it".

BINGO Stevie!

Again, this was the most traumatic event of my entire life. In a flash at the age of 20: No more job. No more immediate or extended family. No more family friends. No future multi-million dollar inheritance. No immediate funds because I'd never touched a penny. And for the previous four years, I'd worked for him for next to nothing to help him establish his business with the promise that he'd well and truly reward me when the business began to make some big money.

The only thing in my favour was that over the coming years, the business kept losing money, long after I was gone—as I knew it would, because I knew exactly what he was doing and why the company was losing money in the first place. And eventually my mother's properties, and so her money, ran out and the business folded.

So people were then able to see that maybe Stevie wasn't as wicked as they'd been told. But by then it was all too late.

The other positive for me is that I now have a great piece of lived-experience, demonstrating **fear-based coercion, and an egocentric lack of courage**, that I can share with you ☺.

You can certainly read the full story in Chapters 11 and 12 of ***Brainwashed***.

Throughout your life, whatever abuse you've experienced, **I guarantee** that there will be a nugget of gold, a life lesson, hiding in there somewhere for you. You just need **to summon the courage to hang on in there and keep digging**.

From my own experience **I KNOW** that you'll have your ups and your downs. So be very kind to yourself. Enjoy the ups and give yourself plenty of self-compassion when those downs come along—and they will.

And no matter what, you just gotta keep searching for the gold—it will be there.

In my Book 3 ~ ***Conscious Self-Discovery,*** I talk a lot more about fear, especially in Chapter 5—"Techniques for Healing".

Activity 2: Cpt 9—Emotionally-based Fears

This is a similar activity to the previous one, but with just a slightly different perspective.

Write down as many "emotionally-based" fears as you can think of that someone, anyone, could possibly have; such as losing their job, losing control of a situation or person.

Mark in some way, perhaps with a highlighter, all of those fears, if any, that you currently have at this general time in your life, or that you've had in the past?

In case they're triggered again in the future, what are you going to do about them?

Characteristics of Courage

One of the reasons that I love studying the ancient philosophers, like Aristotle, is because virtually everything in Aristotle's books applies just as much today as it did all that time ago—ignoring the cultural differences, of course.

And in his book *The Nicomachean Ethics*, back in about 350 BCE, Aristotle, who is often referred to as the father of **Virtue Ethics**, gave some key criteria for defining a moral virtue. Criteria that are still used today including defining Moral Courage.

So the following are the **criteria for developing Moral Courage**.

- **Consciously:** **You** **choose** to act courageously consciously and intentionally, knowing exactly what you're doing. So it can't be something you do by chance.
- **Unconditionally:** **You** must actually **choose** to act courageously without any strings attached. So you choose to do it totally unconditionally, without any ulterior motive such as self-glory or greed.
- **Voluntarily:** **You** must **choose** to act courageously completely voluntarily. Not because anyone has convinced you, or coerced you, to act that way. **You have chosen** to act courageously, completely because **in your heart, you truly believe it's the right thing to do**.

24/7—Habituation: You act courageously 24/7, **when appropriate**, because acting courageously has become a habit. It's part of your character, your identity. It's who you are and how you'd always automatically act in that situation.

However, because **courage is also an intellectual virtue**, it's that side of things that'll help you to determine if a courageous act is indeed appropriate at any specific time.

So you develop your **moral virtues through habituation**, but intellectual virtues, including **intellectual courage**, are acquired and developed over time chiefly through **the combination of education AND life-experience.**

This is a bit like I mentioned at the very start of this chapter when I said you'll really be ready to "change the world" when you have, or have access to, **both life-experience AND multi-perspective academic rigor.**

As an example, **wisdom** is considered to be concerned with universal truths that result when you **combine your intuition with scientific knowledge, or intellectual/academic study**.[31]

On the other hand, **practical knowledge**, which is also known as **prudence (*phronesis*)**, or **today "street smarts",** is to do with **basic practical common-sense** with regard to any particular situation.[32]

And practical knowledge is generally acquired with life-experience, which might even include learning from your mates who've experienced that same situation before you.

Aristotle[33] once said that no matter how much academic knowledge a young person might have, they can never be expected to be prudent (have street-smarts) because they don't have the necessary life experience that only comes with age. One of the many benefits that come with age—*Yaaaaa* 😊

But it's not only young people who lack prudence, or street-smarts. People of any age can be wise, with intuition and scientific knowledge, or intellectual/academic study, and yet have no street smarts if they lack basic common-sense and are unfamiliar with common life-situations.[34]

Many decades ago, I knew an incredibly skilled internationally renowned surgeon who came up with a number of life-changing techniques in his field. But he had no idea that he should occasionally check the oil and water levels in the engine of his very expensive car, as was required back in those days.

Perhaps you too know people who are very wise in their specific field but have a total lack of basic common sense and real life experience.

Or a street kid who has more life-experience than most people will every have. But without some intellectual wisdom, they have no idea how to use their street smarts in the most effective and productive manner.

Activity 3: Cpt 9—People with a Single Skill Set

1. List all the people you can think of who are incredible skilled in just a single side of life, as was the surgeon I just spoke about. So brilliant professionally, but couldn't even change a light bulb, or vice versa.

2. Are you one of those people? If so, how do you get on if the other side of life needs attention?

Finally, there's also a key characteristic of courage that doesn't necessarily apply to other virtues. It's often said that before an act can be considered **courageous, there must be a significant personal threat** either to your physical safety or to your status, or personal comfort in some way. This was evident in virtually all of the examples above.

My Final Comments

In the final chapter of ***Brainwashed***, you'll discover a couple of pages in which I speak directly to each of the main areas of the community that I felt would benefit from reading ***Brainwashed***. I'd now like to direct just one or two sentences to some of those same people.

To …

- **Victim/Survivors:** You're already so **very courageous**, after all you're here. So you must be a survivor. And **surviving takes courage**. So just continue to develop, and hone, and directionalise that heart-centred courage of yours and go out and "make-a-difference" that the world is waiting for you to make.

  And a big **CONGRATULATIONS** for your reminder to the world, with your ad in the 2026 Superbowl. 😊

- **Psychologists & Counsellors:** I trust that you have **the courage** to say: "Although I've been working in this area for a very long time, I know that I'll never have all the answers, which is why I keep on studying".

- **Perpetrators of Psychological Abuse:** It's time to have **the courage** to say: "I know that I need help to better understand and so overcome my heinous actions".

- **Parents of Young Children:** I trust you'll have **the courage** to accept that you don't have all the answers, and neither did/do ***your*** parents.

- **Legislators:** I trust you'll have **the courage** to go against the "party line" if it becomes necessary to do what society really needs.

- **The Media:** I trust that you'll have **the courage** to educate us all about **coercion** and the hidden traumas associated with **emotional/psychological abuse**.

- **Anti-Abuse Advocates:** I thank you so much, and acknowledge **your courage** in doing the wonderful work you do.

Congratulations

It is not enough to know, you must also use the knowledge; it is not enough to wish; you must also act. Thinking in order to act, acting in order to think, that is the sum of all wisdom.

~ Goethe ~

You've now crossed the bridge from Book 7 ~ *Conscious Feminine* ***ENERGY*** — and Lady Phoenix is waiting for you in Book 8 ~ *Conscious Leadership* — sleeves rolled up, ready to pass on her **transformational traits** to guide your own rebirth: becoming the very special and unique hero the world is waiting for... not despite the life you've led, but **because** of the life you've led.

In 1966, Dr. Carroll Quigley[35] argued that our worst tragedies are human-made—and therefore avoidable. We don't have to keep repeating outdated paradigms and negative masculine energy. **We can choose** virtues like: Courage, Compassion, and Love-in-Action — and change our culture.

The world doesn't change through outrage alone. It changes when ordinary people refuse to normalise harm.

Courage is not a feeling.

It's a choice.

And you CAN make it.

Love,

~ Appendix A ~
Your Transformational Journey through The *Conscious Change* Series

Raising Ethical Consciousness in Our World of Relationships

Storytelling is one of the oldest and most powerful transformational tools available to us. That's why all of my books are sprinkled with many different forms of storytelling. And this Appendix uses the metaphoric travel brochure to explain the different ways you can choose to "travel" on your transformational "journey", complete with stop-overs (aka books), as you develop the life-skills to become a **Heart-Centred Conscious Leader of Change**.

It's evident to an ever-growing number of smart, open-minded, heart-weary humans that we're living in a world where all too many unethical people are in positions of power, in all areas of life. These include leaders in the home, the community, the parliament/congress, professionals, and those on the world-stage: making decisions driven by power-hungry greed, ego, ignorance, fear, and outdated paradigms. And it's destroying our planet, our peace, our relationships, our potential, and our inner power.

Due to the life I've led—professionally and experientially—I'm committed to **Raising Ethical Consciousness in Our World**

of Relationships, and so help to create a more Peaceful, Loving, and Sustainable world—but we all need to work together. My contribution primarily comes from The ***Conscious Change Series:*** books, workshops, and coaching.

And there's more than one way to take that transformational **Conscious Change** journey. ...

The Scenic Route — READ ALL 10 BOOKS

The ***Conscious Change Series*** can be read as 10 independent, stand-alone books—each packed with vital insights for **Conscious, Heart-Centred Leaders** and those who aspire to be.

The Guided Tour — YOUR STEP-BY-STEP TRANSFORMATION

The books are arranged in a specific order—Books 1–10—like **stop-overs on a journey**. Your **ultimate transformation peaks in Book 8** (***Conscious Leadership: Born of Heart-Centred Life- Skills and Global Wisdom***), when you'll be ready to lead change in any area of life and make a difference to **YOUR** world—or even **THE** world.

Books 9 and 10 help you to stay mentally and physically strong so you can live a long, happy, and purposeful life as a **Heart-Centred Conscious Leader of Change**.

The Fast-Track Transformation — LIVE THE INSIGHTS

Skip the 10-book reading marathon (or supplement it) with my **12-week online workshop**, **Strategic Heart-Centred Leadership.**

I'll guide you through the key insights from all 10 books—week by week, live on Zoom.

If you'd like to be the first to know when the next transformational workshop will open, just add your name to my mailing list on www.StevieCarnegie.com

The Tailor-Made Path — GROUP COACHING/MASTERMIND

Prefer a more personal, high-touch experience?

Join my **Group Coaching/Mastermind Program: Designing Your Conscious Future**.

An exclusive, invitation only, 6-Month **Group Coaching/Mastermind Experience because...**

A Group Coaching/Mastermind program is a far more powerful, and effective process, with greater transformational outcomes than one-on-one coaching.

Details are at the end of this book, after my bio.

The View from the Top — START AT BOOK 8

You could leap straight to **your "ultimate destination" in Book 8**, skim for the big picture, then circle back to the earlier books in any order you like.

It's like peeking at the last chapter of a mystery novel—except this is non-fiction, so knowing the end makes the beginning ***more*** **meaningful**.

The Only Crisis the World is Facing Is a Leadership Crisis.

YOUR STOP-OVERS ON THE JOURNEY

(Each book in the series is a Transformational "Stop-Over" on your Heart-Centred journey)

Stop-Over 1 ~ Your Transformational Travel Brochure
(Bk 1 ~ Conscious Change for an Ethical Business, Life, and World)

Get your full journey's map—and see why "We not Me" is the change the world needs.

Stop-Over 2 ~ Laying the Foundations for Your Journey ~ Part 1
(Bk 2 ~ Conscious Intelligence Competencies)

Master the 9 Conscious Intelligence Competencies for thriving in an interconnected world of relationships.

Stop-Over 3 ~ Laying the Foundations for Your Journey ~ Part 2
(Bk 3 ~ Conscious Self-Discovery)

Deepen Competencies 1, 2, & 3—self-awareness, self-love—self-compassion, and self-control—the foundation for all conscious growth.

Stop-Over 4 ~ Finding Your North Star
(Bk 4 ~ Conscious Life-Purpose)

Discover your true reason for being—and how to live it every day.

Stop-Over 5 ~ Opening Your Heart & Connecting to the "Universe" ~ Part 1

(Bk 5 ~ Conscious Love)

Lead with the highest vibration of virtue: a love that transforms people and systems.

Stop-Over 6 ~ Opening Your Heart & Connecting to the "Universe" ~ Part 2

(Bk 6 ~ Conscious Gratitude)

Turn gratitude into a daily leadership superpower for joy, resilience, and connection.

Stop-Over 7 ~ Global Understanding & Your Introduction to Lady Phoenix

(Bk 7 ~ Conscious Feminine *ENERGY*)

Understand the global shifts shaping our future—and meet your tour-guide to the new era, Lady Phoenix.

Rising from the ashes of outdated 20th century paradigms at the end of Book 7, LADY PHOENIX is the transformational metaphor for 21st-century Conscious Leadership awakening.

She returns, standing on solid ground on the cover of Book 8, with "sleeves rolled up" [wings removed], ready to get to work and guide your transformational triumph, as a Heart-Centred Conscious Leader of Change, with Courage, Compassion, Creativity, and Conscious Intelligence.

The Bridge-7a ~ The Bridge from Stop-Over 7—Preparing You For Your Transformation during Stop-Over 8 on the other side

(Bk 7a ~ From Coercion to Courage)

Whether you've experienced past pain, or abuse, or not, once you cross the bridge you'll understand that success is possible not despite of your past, but BECAUSE of your past, so you'll be ready for your Transformational Ascension during your next Stop-Over.

In the unlikely even that you have no past pain, please just enjoy the beautiful view from either side of the bridge as you walk across to Stop-Over 8.

Stop-Over 8 ~ Your Transformational Ascension with Lady Phoenix

(Bk 8 ~ Conscious Leadership)

With Lady Phoenix at your side, develop your full leadership potential—ready to make the difference only you can.

Stop-Over 9 ~ Your Life as a Heart-Centred, "Conscious" Leader of Change ~ Part 1

(Bk 9 ~ Conscious Happiness 101)

Make happiness a habit with mental wellbeing through play, laughter, mindfulness, and positive psychology.

Stop-Over 10 ~ Your Life as a Heart-Centred, "Conscious" Leader of Change ~ Part 2
(Bk 10 ~ Conscious Longevity)

Achieve physical wellbeing for a longer healthier, and more purposeful life.

THE PREQUEL

The Anatomy; The Antidote & The Bridge

Brainwashed: The True Story of Psychological Domestic Abuse and the PTSD Aftermath – Winner of 10 International Awards—**exposes the Anatomy of Abuse**.

Conscious Leadership (Book 8) **delivers the Antidote to Abuse**—preventing it through **Courage, Compassion, Creativity,** and **Conscious Intelligence.**

Where will you begin?

Choose your route.

Take your journey.

And join us as a

Heart-Centred Conscious Leader of Change.

Here's a slight adaptation of Andrew Carnegie's principles for success, as related by Napoleon Hill[1]:

> When the [ten Conscious Change Books] are blended together, like the links of a chain, this combination leads to the development of stupendous power which cannot be attained by just the individual application of any one of them.

With your Transformational Journey in mind, I invite you to think of Book 1, as a **Travel Brochure for your Journey, where, if you so choose, you'll awaken at the end of Book 8 as a Heart-Centred Conscious Leader of Change,** with even **higher levels of Consciousness than you might already have.**

Time is Now

to embark on your transformational journey.

But of course the

Choice is Yours

and so

It's Up to You

whether you join us or not.

[1] Napoleon Hill. 1945/1965. *The Master-Key to Riches*. Fawcett Crest Books. P 38.

Endnotes

1 https://www.pbs.org/newshour/politics/7-things-to-know-about-the-justice-departments-epstein-files

2 The contents of this table have been adapted from numerous resources including Chat GPT and a Google AI deep search.

3 "It's like déjà vu all over again" is attributed to New York Yankees Hall of Fame catcher Yogi Berra, not the cartoon character Yogi Bear. The quote is widely believed to have originated around 1961 when Berra witnessed teammates Mickey Mantle and Roger Maris hitting back-to-back home runs.

4 This list has been adapted from https://www.relationshipsvictoria.org.au/news/what-is-coercive-control/

5 https://www.nsw.gov.au/family-and-relationships/coercive-control/what-are-impacts. Plus The New South Wales Domestic Violence Death Review Team, Report 2021-2023.

6 Jeglic Ph.D. Elizabeth L. (2021) "What Everyone Needs to Understand About Sexual Coercion". *Psychology Today*. March 8th, 2021. https://www.psychologytoday.com/us/blog/protecting-children-from-sexual-abuse/202103/what-everyone-needs-to-understand-about-sexual

7 I put both terms mediator/conciliator for two reasons. First, at different times I've worked as both a mediator and also as a conciliator. The other reason is that there are slight differences in the roles of a mediator and a conciliator in the States versus Australia.

8 In Chapter 4, Bk #3, see the subtitle "Your Attachment Pattern & Relationships".

9 The dentist's name is Sharonne Zaks, and her interview was on "The Conversation"- Radio National, Thu 25 Dec 2025 at 3:00pm, https://www.abc.net.au/listen/programs/conversations/rn-sharonne-zaks-rpt-summer/106152274

10 Wikipedia—***Access Hollywood* tape. 2006.** "Transcript: "... Taped Comments About Women". *The New York Times*. October 8, 2016. Retrieved November 30, 2023.

[11] The Young Turks ~ "Thomas Massie: This Is The EPSTEIN Administration" Major Cover up. February 16th, 2026 https://www.youtube.com/watch?v=lfP3G6GGNXA

[12] "Department of Justice Publishes 3.5 Million Responsive Pages in Compliance with the Epstein Files Transparency Act": Friday, January 30, 2026. https://www.justice.gov/opa/pr/department-justice-publishes-35-million-responsive-pages-compliance-epstein-files

[13] "More than 3 million files related to Epstein released by DOJ". January 31st, 2026. https://www.cbc.ca/player/play/video/9.7068642

[14] Dr G Explains ~ Is Epstein Alive? New Epstein Escape Plan Files Found! Forensic Expert Analysis. February 8th, 2026. https://www.youtube.com/watch?v=qSKeLdtBY-4

[15] Mario Nawfal ~ "Made A Decoy Body!" - Forensic Expert On Epstein Buying Babies, Prison Cameras, Codewords & More..." ~ Made a Fake Body February 16th, 2026. https://www.youtube.com/watch?v=kiSOoxmALqo

[16] "Diabolical: The Epstein Files". A documentary screened on Australian ABC on March 2nd, 2026. ABC News Documentary Production. 2026. https://iview.abc.net.au/show/diabolical-the-epstein-files/video/NS2625H001S00

[17] Congressman Jared Moskowitz (D) of Florida, interviewed on CNN. "Congressman reveals what he saw in the unredacted Epstein files". https://www.youtube.com/watch?v=LgHXF0_HOm4

[18] BBC, online: February 8th, 2026. Andy Verity. "Andrew shared confidential information with Epstein as trade envoy, files suggest". https://www.bbc.com/news/articles/c99j01p1yjro

[19] Daily Mail. February 10th, 2026. "Buckingham Palace says it is ready to support the police in any Andrew probe as King expresses his 'profound concern'". https://www.dailymail.co.uk/news/article-15544277/Palace-says-ready-support-police-Andrew-probe.html

[20] BBC online News. "Police investigate Mandelson over claims he leaked information to Epstein" Joshua Nevett, and Harry Farley. 4 February 2026. https://www.bbc.com/news/articles/cre2yqyex4zo

[21] These are just some of the numerous websites discussing what they've found in the Epstein Files linking Epstein to many countries around the world.

* PBS. Feb 11, 2026. "New revelations from Epstein files take a toll across Europe" https://www.pbs.org/newshour/world/new-revelations-from-epstein-files-take-a-toll-across-europe

* Edgaras Savickas. 06 Feb 2026, "Epstein's money trail in Lithuania: dozens of bank transfers since 2008" https://www.lrt.lt/en/news-in-english/19/2828150/epstein-s-money-trail-in-lithuania-dozens-of-bank-transfers-since-2008

* I've Had It Podcast and You Tube.* https://edition.cnn.com/2026/02/08/politics/epstein-putin-russian-officials-connections

* https://www.aljazeera.com/economy/2026/2/12/epstein-sought-help-of-ex-russian-official-linked-to-fsb-files-show

* https://www.aljazeera.com/video/the-listening-post/2026/2/9/the-anatomy-of-the-epstein-network

*https://www.aljazeera.com/news/2026/2/9/what-were-jeffrey-epsteins-links-to-israel

[22] The Sascha Riley Interview Information. Allegedly, there is ample supporting evidence including pornography films, and videos. Allegedly there's a military report involving the court-martial of a fellow soldier found with child pornography depicting Sascha and one of the alleged murder victims when they were both children. Much of the evidence has been suppressed, although some is allegedly obtainable by FOIA request, and by investigator request.

[23] Piers Morgan Uncensored 'You Talk UTTER Sh*t!' Piers Morgan LOSES It Over Epstein Claims | "Royal Family Could Be Swept Out" c February 14th, 2026. https://www.youtube.com/watch?v=cfYtqzrjCgo

[24] https://en.wikipedia.org/wiki/Lady_Victoria_Hervey

[25] https://www.youtube.com/watch?v=kf_lvLxa8lc "New photos from Epstein files appears to show Andrew on all fours over female | BBC News". 4,565,093 views Feb 1, 2026 #Epstein #BBCNews Pictures showing Andrew Mountbatten-Windsor kneeling on all

fours over a female lying on the ground. These are part of the latest release of documents related to the late sex offender Jeffrey Epstein.

[26] " Roy Moore sexual misconduct" allegations. https://en.wikipedia.org/wiki/Roy_Moore_sexual_misconduct_allegations

[27] "Epstein's ghost is haunting the UK" *If You're Interested*. Australian ABC TV. February 20th, 2026.

[28]"She accused him of rape, but Prince Andrew's downfall is too late for Virginia Roberts Giuffre". Tessa Flemming. Sat 1 Nov 2025. ABC News website. https://www.abc.net.au/news/2025-11-01/virginia-giuffre-voice-finally-heard-prince-andrew-epstein-fight/105957478

[29] Helliwell, Layard, and Sachs, 2013

[30] The Nuremberg defense, or "superior orders" is a legal plea claiming a defendant is not guilty of war crimes because they were merely following orders from a superior. Primarily used by Nazi leaders during the 1945–1946 during Nuremberg trials, **this defense was rejected by the tribunal**, establishing that **individuals have a moral duty to disobey illegal orders**.

[31] NE: Book 6—1140b33-1141a19

[32] Thomson, 1976:209,212

[33] NE: 1142a01-20

[34] NE: 1141b1-15

[35] Carroll Quigley was a professor of history at Georgetown University from 1941 to 1976. He also taught at Princeton and Harvard, and lectured at the Brookings Institution. He was a frequent lecturer at the U.S. Naval Weapons Laboratory, the Foreign Service Institute, and the Naval College at Norfolk, Virginia. In 1958, he served as a consultant to the Congressional Select Committee that set up the National Space Agency.

URL "Bibliography"

WARNING

The following websites support information contained in Chapter 6 ~ The Epstein Files and Chapter 7 ~ What Would YOU Have Done... *REALLY???*. However, I found the content on a lot of the following videos to be very upsetting, and you might too. So you might think twice about watching or listening to them.

- Congressman Ro Khanna (D) on IHIP (I've Had It video podcast) speaking with Jennifer Welch ~ "Rep. DROPS BOMB on Trump After Seeing UNREDACTED Files! "The Famous Names are HORRIFIC" February 14th, 2026. https://www.youtube.com/watch?v=vHqnK0nfiSo&list=PLByI_Pnh1ah_lGu2J5HwQpZakL346p_89&index=23
- The Trump Report "Trump's Epstein 'coverup' is starting to unravel" | Professor David Cay Johnston, Feb 13th, 2026. https://www.youtube.com/watch?v=cFMqbhWdtIk&list=PLGeQKoGUstRA9Zv-J_Qdc9Ldrcea-HdrD&index=3
- Congressman Jared Moskowitz (D) of Florida, interviewed on CNN. "Congressman reveals what he saw in the unredacted Epstein files" February 10th, 2026. https://www.youtube.com/watch?v=LgHXF0_HOm4
- The Young Turks ~ "Thomas Massie: This Is The EPSTEIN Administration" Major Cover up. February 16th, 2026. https://www.youtube.com/watch?v=lfP3G6GGNXA
- Ari Melber, Journalist & Attorney: "When did he know? Melber on Trump's early knowledge of Epstein, 'evil' Maxwell (per FBI FILE)"February 10th, 2026. https://www.youtube.com/watch?v=m7uprFFXPw4
- Moon ~ "Epstein had dirt on everyone - and that's why he was untouchable" February 10th, 2026. https://www.msn.com/en-gb/news/world/epstein-had-dirt-on-everyone-and-that-s-why-he-was-untouchable/vi-AA1VJQBs?ocid=BingNewsSerp
- PBS ~ "New revelations from Epstein files take a toll across Europe" February 11th, 2026.

https://www.pbs.org/newshour/world/new-revelations-from-epstein-files-take-a-toll-across-europe

- The Listening Post ~ "The anatomy of the Epstein network" ~ February 9th, 2026. https://www.aljazeera.com/video/the-listening-post/2026/2/9/the-anatomy-of-the-epstein-network
- Aljazeera: John Power ~ "Epstein sought help of ex-Russian official linked to FSB, files show" February 12th, 2026. https://www.aljazeera.com/economy/2026/2/12/epstein-sought-help-of-ex-russian-official-linked-to-fsb-files-show
- Daily Mail ~ "Buckingham Palace says it is ready to support the police in any Andrew probe as King expresses his 'profound concern" February 10th, 2026. https://www.dailymail.co.uk/news/article-15544277/Palace-says-ready-support-police-Andrew-probe.html
- Aljazeera: Simon Speakman Cordall ~ "What were Jeffrey Epstein's links to Israel?" February 9th, 2026. https://www.aljazeera.com/news/2026/2/9/what-were-jeffrey-epsteins-links-to-israel
- CNN Politics: Isabelle Khurshudyan, Zahra Ullah, Austin Culpepper ~ "Epstein tried to cozy up to Russian officials, including Putin, documents show" February 8th, 2026. https://edition.cnn.com/2026/02/08/politics/epstein-putin-russian-officials-connections
- LRT.lt: Edgaras Savickas ~ "Epstein's money trail in Lithuania: dozens of bank transfers since 2008" February 6th, 2026. https://www.lrt.lt/en/news-in-english/19/2828150/epstein-s-money-trail-in-lithuania-dozens-of-bank-transfers-since-2008
- True Crime Recaps ~ "The disturbing truth about Jeffrey Epstein" ~ mid December 2025. https://www.msn.com/en-au/news/other/the-disturbing-truth-about-jeffrey-epstein/vi-A1RI8Vj?ocid=winp2fptaskbarhover&cvid=698904a04be64bb99356be7851461878&ei=14#:~:text=The%20disturbing%20truth,23
- ABC News ~ "Poland to probe links between Epstein and Russian intelligence". February 4th, 2026. https://www.abc.net.au/news/2026-02-04/epstein-russian-intelligence-links-poland-investigation/106302296
- Epstein's Austrian passport. https://www.youtube.com/watch?v=TtxGJdS5jSo

- Dr G Explains ~ "New Epstein Files: Agent Epstein, Sulfuric Acid, and Redactions Forensic Expert Analysis" February 14th, 2026. https://www.youtube.com/watch?v=w75a4A_BnpI
- TV Talk ~ "DEAD Bodies' In Epstein Files? Royal Author Claims CHILLING New Revelations To Come" February 12th, 2026. https://www.youtube.com/watch?v=3Wvg1Z187kM
- Novara Media ~ "Epstein's SICK Messages To Billionaire REVEALED" – "I Loved Torture Video" email viewed. February 15th, 2026. https://www.youtube.com/watch?v=j2JRuEQWq-c
- Trap More Ross ~ "Epstein's Driver Confessed to 2 Bodies..." February 8th, 2026. https://www.youtube.com/watch?v=ZGe5_jX6Ido
- Novara Media ~ "The SICKEST Epstein Email" ~ Kill the Poor. February 7th, 2026. https://www.youtube.com/watch?v=wzGyRyeC4IE
- Mario Nawfal ~ "Made A Decoy Body!" - Forensic Expert On Epstein Buying Babies, Prison Cameras, Codewords & More..." ~ Made a Fake Body February 16th, 2026. https://www.youtube.com/watch?v=kiSOoxmALqo
- Shaun Attwood ~ "Is Epstein STILL ALIVE? EXAMINED by Blood Analyst Jeffrey Gentry" February 16th, 2026. https://www.youtube.com/watch?v=ACereyRILZo
- Volksgeist ~ "The Horrifying Origins of Jeffery Epstein" February 3rd, 2026. https://www.youtube.com/watch?v=JPbQnmbXWJ4
- The Free Press ~ "I Watched 14 Hours of Epstein Videos. Here's What I Saw" February 10th, 2026. https://www.youtube.com/watch?v=NChzPbfykcY
- Jack Cocchiarella ~ "FINALLY! Marjorie Posts Epstein Evidence Trump Feared MOST" Majorie Taylor Greene. February 11th, 2026. https://www.youtube.com/watch?v=-FJ2uJUBF7s
- Sabby Sabs ~ "What HAPPENED To Sascha Riley?" ~ Who is Sascha Riley? The Man who's come forward claiming he was raped by Epstein and his playmates when he was a little boy. February 24th, 2026. https://www.youtube.com/watch?v=oMjCq5u2FTg
- Shaun Attwood ~ "EPSTEIN FILES Did PRINCESS Give Birth To Epstein's Child? NORWAYS ROYAL FAMILY SCANDAL" February 6th, 2026.

  https://www.youtube.com/watch?v=tzvxGYzrWO4

- The Daily Beast Podcast with Joanna Coles ~ "Why Trump Is Putting King Charles in Grave Danger" February 9th, 2026. Steve Schmidt warning King Charles not to visit America in 2026. https://www.youtube.com/watch?v=o4AvSBmy7zA&list=PLByI_Pnh1ah-M7lfkQsdjRnjLCZ-Bfpwa
- "A Message From A Male Survivor of Epstein Island" Mid-February 2026. https://www.youtube.com/watch?v=a7L4B5NgeKI
- Matt Cullen. "The MISSING Epstein Boy: The Story Donald Trump DOES NOT Want Us To Hear" Mid-February, 2026. https://www.youtube.com/watch?v=C2ZAMJz_xMA
- Carly P Reilly. "Epstein + the Rothschilds: What We Know" March 4th, 2026. https://www.youtube.com/watch?v=Np5gdqCR0R4
- Interesting details as to why the public no longer trust what they are being told, leading to conspiracies, all due to a total lack of transparency. "FOUND Madeleine McCann in the Epstein Files? The 2026 Bombshell Nobody Expected". True Crime Noir. March 3rd, 2026. https://www.youtube.com/watch?v=xF_4ItkOjzk
- "Madeleine McCann in the Epstein Files?" True Crime. Crime Noir. March 3rd, 2026. https://www.youtube.com/watch?v=xF_4ItkOjzk&t=18s
- This video says it all. Franzese Wines. "The Epstein Files Are A Distraction (Here's What They Are Hiding)". February 4th, 2026. https://www.youtube.com/watch?v=-nZPkD-ncqc

~ Stevie's Story ~

Dr. Stevie Carnegie

PhD; MSc; MA; BA (Hons)

Conscious Leadership Ethicist, Moral Philosopher, & Multi-Award-Winning Author

Raising Ethical Consciousness in Our World of Relationships

Dr. Stevie Carnegie is a Moral Philosopher with an extensive Behavioural Science background, a PhD in the **Ethics of Conscious Leadership**, and the author of the Multi-Award-Winning ***Conscious Change Series*** **of 10 books** and their prequel, ***Brainwashed***.

With over 40 years at the forefront of Heart-Centred Conscious (Ethical) Leadership, Stevie has **broken barriers** as Australia's first female oil company field executive, where her duties were those of a **business coach** long before the term "business coach" was ever even thought of. She also based that coaching work exclusively on **conscious business** and **conscious leadership** strategies, before the "conscious" label was ever thought of for that sort of thing either. And the results could not have been better.

She then took that pioneering mindset into her own enterprise, becoming the franchisee of the first 24-hour self-service "service station" in her state. With **one bold decision**, she immediately led the way, transforming the service station's shop into a thriving 24-hour gift store by replacing the traditional dirty car maintenance products, with everything from chocolates and toys to artisan clocks and vases. The shop became her million dollar-plus site's most profitable division, **sparking a trend quickly adopted nationwide**.

Stevie went on to **transform lives** with her conversations as an award-winning capital city talk-radio broadcaster. Then with the integration of her two great passions—Heart-Centred Conscious Leadership and Behavioural Science—she **shaped future leaders** by teaching MBA Leadership students in Australia, Hong Kong, and Singapore.

During her time in Singapore, she also designed and delivered regular Ecotourism Interpretation workshops for the Singapore National Parks Board. These classes were held in Singapore's beautiful National Parks. And as many of her classes were held in the open, Stevie loves to share the story of her special students, **the macaque monkeys,** who joined in while watching intently from the trees above.

Today, her greatest passion is **igniting the magic** and **boundaryless possibilities** that transforms individuals into **Heart-Centred Conscious Leaders of Change**—leaders who then inspire transformation in everyone they connect with. All of them contributing to **a world of Peace, Love, and Sustainability**.

You can find out more on

https://www.steviecarnegie.com/stevies-story

Stevie is also the victim/survivor of numerous forms of psychological abuse and some physical abuse. She strongly believes that rebirth and success is possible not DESPITE of your past life, but BECAUSE of it.

Testimonial from Master of Environmental Management Classes in Singapore

… Dr Carnegie is entertaining, creative and innovative and makes people laugh. … Her class is often filled with cheer and smiling faces. I can still remember one lecture where she dressed up as a clown, and the classroom was decorated with colourful balloons, ornaments, and surrounded with music. Scattered around were tidbits, lollies, and sweet-smelling incense. We were indeed pleasantly surprised when we entered the room and saw the well-decorated environment. We were even more surprised when we were asked to follow her actions, by dancing around the room and climbing over and under the furniture. During this 5-10 mins exercise, Dr Carnegie did so much in bringing across her point that people are more receptive to different senses and they learn through their senses. This must have been a memorable occasion for many of us, as we (her students in Singapore) still talked about it whenever we happened to meet or discuss issues related to Ecotourism and Interpretation skills.

… Dr Carnegie continues to ask pertinent questions until she finds satisfactory answers. She is well-versed with environmental issues and is able to deliver thought-provoking information that stimulates our minds and influences our actions and values. She is a remarkable person and based on her stories, she practices what she preaches, both at work and in her home.

… I find Dr Carnegie to be a wonderful person to talk to, and to work with. As an educator and trainer, she is inspiring, caring and willing to share her knowledge and experiences with others…

Mr WONG, Tuan Wah
Director (Conservation)
National Parks Board

YOUR LIFE-CHANGING *CONSCIOUS CHANGE* SHORTCUT

*Skip the ten-book reading marathon and **experience** the insights live, week-by-week because ...*

You're Here to Make a Real Difference—Heart First

and so

Dr Stevie Carnegie offers two rare and powerful opportunities to bring your soul's work into the world and ***become a Conscious Hero the world is waiting for.***

THE WORKSHOP:

Strategic Heart-Centred Leadership

A Life-Changing 12-Week Online Workshop

Your shortcut to the soul-deep shifts no book alone can give.

- Courageously explore the key points in the 10-book Conscious Change Series through powerful live Zoom sessions with Dr Stevie Carnegie herself.
- You'll awaken your **Strategic Heart-Centred Power**—with Courage, Compassion, Creativity, Curiosity PLUS Conscious Intelligence—to lead meaningful change, in all areas of your life or business: leading from the heart.
  - ✓ *Prerequisites:* An Open Heart, a Commitment to Change, and a Curious and Open Mind.
  - ✓ Run 1-2 times a year.
  - ✓ Open to all.
  - ✓ Be among the first to hear about the next round by joining Stevie's mailing list on https://www.StevieCarnegie.com

The Group Coaching/Mastermind Program:

Designing Your Conscious Future

An exclusive, invitation only, 6-Month Group Coaching/ Mastermind Experience because ...

A well facilitated Group Coaching/Mastermind program is a far more powerful, and effective process, with greater transformational outcomes than one-on-one coaching.

So ...

Join Dr Stevie Carnegie in a Zoom circle of no more than ten.

- ❖ You'll go far beyond goal setting.
- ❖ You'll design the life you were born to live. A life that's in harmony with your ***heart's deepest knowing***—one aligned with purpose, peace, power, and profound impact.
- ❖ You'll unlock your boundaryless magic, break free from old limiting stories, align with your true purpose, and step fully into your next chapter as a **Conscious Leader of Change**—a life you can't wait to live.

This is transformation by design, *but only if you're ready.*

- ✓ Maximum of 10 participants per group, by application.
- ✓ Maximum of 4 groups run each year.
- ✓ Rich, unfiltered discussions, and tailored feedback.
- ✓ Includes a customised version of the ***Strategic Heart-Centred Leadership*** workshop.
- ✓ **Your Investment**: *From* $10,000 USD

Email your expression of interest to: Support@StevieCarnegie.com
Subject line: *Designing Your Conscious Future*

The only crisis the world is facing is a Leadership Crisis

The future is calling you now—*Heart First*

The Prequel to the *Conscious Change Series*

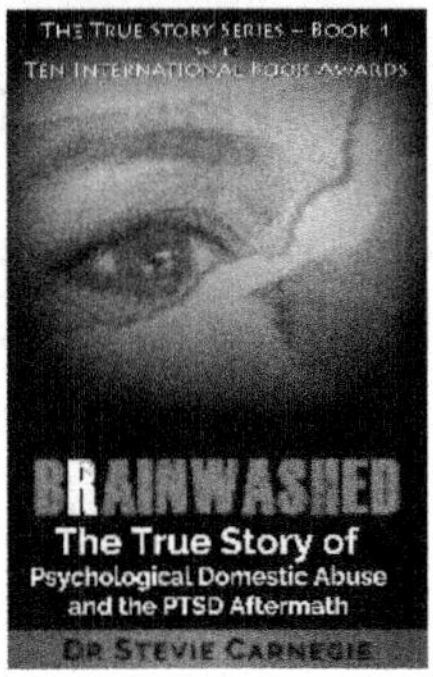

A True Story of Survival and the Science Behind It

Psychological Abuse, including coercive control, gaslighting, weaponizing niceness, and insidious brainwashing is one of the most misunderstood epidemics of our time, whether perpetrated in an office, a church, a school, the community, or a family home. It leaves no visible scars, yet it can lead to disastrous, even deadly, decisions, lasting trauma, physical brain damage, and full-blown PTSD, unless it's **named, understood,** and **healed**.

As a survivor of psychological abuse, Dr Stevie Carnegie, realised the only way to help the public understand this hidden plague was to expose it as she told her own story. Courageously, she did this in ***Brainwashed: The True Story of Psychological Domestic Abuse and the PTSD Aftermath*** blending raw personal storytelling with decades of behavioural science research to shatter myths and answer the real WHY questions including:

- Why people can't "just leave".
- Why trauma can result in brain damage;
- Why psychological trauma can be fatal.

Brainwashed takes you inside the anatomy of toxic power. Yet the same abusive patterns seen destroying a childhood, or a marriage, can also poison a business, an organisation, a community, or an entire culture.

So ***Brainwashed*** is not only Stevie's personal liberation—it's a rallying cry for **recognition, understanding,** and **change** because Stevie's story is true for more people than is realised.

***And if Brainwashed* exposes the Anatomy of abuse...**

... *Conscious Leadership:* delivers the Antidote

At a time when toxic power, fraying trust, and psychological abuse destroy lives, livelihoods, and legacies, this ground-breaking book reveals what most leadership books leave out: the ethics behind behaviour, power, and relationships.

With warmth, humour, and visionary insight, leadership ethicist, Dr. Stevie Carnegie, blends hard-hitting behavioural science, cutting-edge ethical theory and analyses, lived experience, and soul-deep wisdom to expose society's silent epidemic tearing people, systems, organisations, and even countries apart.

The Only Crisis the World is Facing Is a Leadership Crisis.

Conscious Leadership (Book #8 in the Conscious Change Series) reveals **Conscious Heart-Centred Life-Skills**—not domination, power-hungry greed and ego, and outdated paradigms.

More than a leadership book, this is **a relationship requirement** that **rewrites the rules.** A courageous blueprint for **Raising Ethical Consciousness in Our World of Relationships**, unveiling Conscious Leadership Life-Skills in all areas of life—personal, professional, political, and planetary. And it's led by **Lady Phoenix**, the transformational metaphor for **Heart-Centred *Conscious* Leadership Awakening.**

Rising from the ashes of outdated 20th-century paradigms at the end of Book 7, Lady Phoenix returns, standing on solid ground on the cover of Book 8, with "sleeves rolled up" [wings removed], ready to get to work and guide your transformational triumph, as a Heart-Centred Conscious Leader of Change, with **Courage, Compassion, Creativity,** and **Conscious Intelligence**.

Thank you so much for reading the book.

I hope it gave you some fresh insights, and that you would like to help spread these very important messages far and wide.

If so, **please tell your friends, family, & mailing lists** about the book and also post a note on your blogs and social media feeds, **letting your followers know** that they can

Download Their FREE E-Book Now

Bk 1 ~ Conscious Change for an Ethical Business, Life, and World:

An Introduction to Conscious *We not Me* Change and the Conscious Change Series in Review

when they go to

https://www.StevieCarnegie.com

And Do Remember…

to sign up for ***YOUR*** **FREE** downloadable copy of

Bk 1 ~ Conscious Change for an Ethical Business, Life, and World

PLUS the latest Conscious Change News.

Again, just go to my main website.

https://www.StevieCarnegie.com

And because Amazon promotes a book largely based on reviews, if you're an Amazon customer, I'd really appreciate you leaving a review on the book's Amazon page.

You can go to this link now to leave your review.

https://tinyurl.com/book7a

Many Thanks

Printed in Dunstable, United Kingdom

79945139R00097